Creating
Groups

Second Edition

SAGE HUMAN SERVICES GUIDES

A series of books edited by ARMAND LAUFFER and CHARLES D. GARVIN. Published in cooperation with the University of Michigan School of Social Work and other organizations.

Creating Groups

Second Edition

Harvey J. Bertcher
Frank F. Maple

SHSG SAGE HUMAN SERVICES GUIDES 2

Published in cooperation with the University of Michigan School of Social Work

SAGE Publications
International Educational and Professional Publisher
Thousand Oaks   London   New Delhi

Copyright © 1996 by Sage Publications, Inc.

For information address:

SAGE Publications, Inc.
2455 Teller Road
Thousand Oaks, California 91320
E-mail: order@sagepub.com

SAGE Publications Ltd.
6 Bonhill Street
London EC2A 4PU
United Kingdom

SAGE Publications India Pvt. Ltd.
M-32 Market
Greater Kailash I
New Delhi 110 048 India

Printed in the United States of America

Library of Congress Cataloging-in-Publication Data

Bertcher, Harvey J.
     Creating groups / authors, Harvey J. Bertcher and Frank F. Maple.—
     2nd ed.
          p. cm. — (Sage human services guides; v. 2)
     Includes bibliographical references.
     ISBN 0-8039-5491-3 (acid-free paper). — ISBN 0-8039-5492-1 (pbk.:
     acid-free paper).
          1. Small groups—Programmed instruction. 2. Decision-making,
     Group—Programmed Instruction. 3. Social group work—Programmed
     instruction. I. Maple, Frank F. II. Title. III. Series.
     HM133.B478   1996
     302.3'4'077—dc20   95-50168

This book is printed on acid-free paper.

96 97 98 99 10 9 8 7 6 5 4 3 2 1

Sage Production Editor: Tricia K. Bennett

To Gloria Bertcher, my best beloved, 1929-1995
—Harvey J. Bertcher

To Loree Maple, my supportive wife
and companion in life's journey
—Frank F. Maple

CONTENTS

PREFACE

By the time the first edition of this book went to the publishers, it had gone through six major revisions and, frankly, we were tired. What had begun (for H. Bertcher) as an effort to learn how to write a piece of programmed instruction (starting from a one-page handout listing thumbnail sketches of 15 potential group members that had been created by F. Maple as a discussion kickoff) had expanded, grown, changed, been expanded again, been tried out with students, and been further rewritten. In short order, however, we began to think of other issues that should have been discussed. Clearly, another rewrite was needed—someday.

Now we have been given the opportunity to bring the book up-to-date. Before we began to rewrite, we interviewed a number of practitioners and students to learn about the issues they faced when creating groups. From these interviews we realized that in the first edition we had not addressed the impact of organizational realities that affect, and often impede, the process of group creation. Factors of race and gender needed greater attention as did the empowerment of potential members in the composition process. More important was a decision to enlarge the scope of the book to cover all of the aspects that go into the creation of a group, from the germ of an idea to start a group all the way through to planning for and conducting a first meeting in which a facilitator literally creates a group starting with a collection of strangers—that is, people who do not know one another or (as often happens on committees, for example) who do know one another but have not worked together in this particular constellation of membership.

Over the years, several authors have added to knowledge about group composition, and we wanted to include their thinking. Some of this thinking dealt with direct practice, and some of it focused on research. In any event, we decided it was time to pull it together in this second edition, realizing that—even as we wrote—new and relevant knowledge was being created.

It is hoped that the result will provide a full picture of the many ways in which the creation of a group can be planned for, and dealt with, to the benefit of group members.

As with the first edition, we have used our own version of a programmed instruction format—one that requires you to actively respond throughout your reading of this book. If this book belongs to you, we hope that you write your responses wherever they are called for. If you have a library copy, you should have a notebook at hand and write your responses in it. The point is, you will get a great deal more out of this book if you go along with our format and (you guessed it!) write your responses to the questions we pose. Just thinking of a response will not work: Write it down!

In this second edition, we express our appreciation to students and practitioners who were interviewed to learn about their current experiences with group creation. These include Kathy Skilton, Tony Alvarez, and countless others from whom we have learned about group creation in the context of agency realities. We also thank one of our former students, Deborah Fishman, for having provided feedback on an earlier version of the book. Jesse Gordon, a colleague from the School of Social Work's faculty, encouraged us to include content on groups on the Internet, and we thank him for keeping us up-to-date. Robert Bertcher provided a valuable editorial review of the manuscript. Finally, we particularly express our appreciation to our colleagues Charles Garvin and Armand Lauffer, coeditors of the **Sage Human Services Guide** series—Charles because he proposed enlarging this work to encompass the full range of issues associated with group creation and Armand for his editing help and guidance and for his genius in creating this entire **Sage Human Services Guide** series.

1

DEALING WITH DIFFERENCE

Welcome! Let's get started. You are about to read a book that has been written using a "programmed instruction" format. After you read some content, you will be asked questions about that content, then the answer we consider correct will be displayed so you can check your understanding of the material we have presented. This may be different from most of the books you read these days, but we think it facilitates the learning process.

The format for this book is different, and it is this very fact of "difference" that we have chosen as the place to start our discussion of group creation.

Suppose you drive to work every day along a particular route (or, if you are lucky, walk to work because work is close to home). On a particular day, you find your passage blocked by some unexpected road construction, and you face a detour that looks confusing as well as demanding more time than you are accustomed to devoting to this trip.

Question: Which of the following would represent your state of mind at that point?

    A. You would be pleased to have this opportunity to have your routine disrupted so you can experience the demands of a new and unfamiliar route.

    B. You would prefer to have the barrier removed so you can proceed on your accustomed route.

Response: (Please circle your preferred answer and then turn the page to find our preferred answer.)   A   or   B

Answer: You probably answered B.

If you chose A (being a free soul), just look at how you reacted when you found this page was positioned in a way that was not what you expected—that is, was different from what you had presumed you would find—when you turned the page. (We are trying to make a point about difference and promise this will be the last page in this book that is upside down. We deliberately had it printed this way to make our point: People like predictability and generally prefer that things remain the way they have been in the past, that is, the "known way.")

If you are thinking about creating a group, and the use of groups has been a regular part of your agency's operations for some time, then, in a sense, using a group to accomplish some purpose is the known way of doing things. If you are creating a group where groups have not been used before, have not been used regularly, or have not been used for some time, however, then you are creating a difference, and you can expect that people will react (as people—even professionals—are wont to do) with a natural amount of resistance to the changes produced by your project.

In this chapter, we will discuss the predictable and natural resistance you can expect, rather than being surprised that it occurs (which is what many practitioners report). This chapter describes what you need to do to cope with this resistance so that it does not impede your efforts to get your group started. To state it in more positive terms, the chapter deals with what you can do to create an "environment of acceptance"[1] for your efforts.

You may be reading this book because someone (a professor, a supervisor, etc.) has told you that you must (or at least, should) do so, or you may have sought it out to help you in creating a new group. Certainly, we do not want to discourage you from engaging in group creation.

Question: Which of the following represents who you are?

    A. Someone who enjoys a challenge and who believes this group is worth creating.

    B. Someone who would prefer to avoid the extra effort that creating this group will entail.

Response: (circle one)   A   or   B

We hope you chose A. (If you chose B, you may want to abandon plans to create this group.)

ACCEPTANCE ENVIRONMENT

By "acceptance," we mean that administrators and other staff will give active support to your project, and that you will have adequate resources to develop this group. Included in these resources will be your time—that is, your supervisor will see what you are doing as a legitimate use of your time and will (given your other responsibilities) make it possible for you to work on this project. Put simply, some of the right folk think that what you are planning to do or how you are planning to do it, or both, are on the right track.

Question: True or false: Creating an environment of acceptance will require a considerable amount of work on your part.

Response: (circle one)   True   or   False

Most of the time, the answer is true. There may be, at the outset, indifference to your project. There may also be active opposition, in which case you will find yourself working very hard to overcome it.

To create an environment of acceptance, the following must be achieved:

1. Consensus on the purposes of this project among key players in your agency
2. Active support of administrators and staff for the operation of this project
3. Consensus on who or what the target population of this project should be
4. Financial support for this project's budgetary needs

The rest of this chapter will focus on these four components of acceptance.

CONSENSUS ON PURPOSE

Question: Which of the following do you think is the best way to achieve a consensus among administrators, staff, and other interested persons about the purposes[2] of a newly proposed group?

   A. Keep quiet about what you are trying to accomplish so that as few people as possible are aware of your project and you can sneak it in unnoticed.
   B. Discuss your proposal with your supervisor, with fellow staff, with relevant administrators, and anyone else who might become involved with this project.

Response: (circle one)   A   or   B

In our view, you do not build consensus by talking to yourself, so we prefer B. There is a step that should precede consensus building, however, and that is: Create a one-page (or less) statement of purpose that makes sense to you. In other words, before approaching others, you need to do some homework so that you know what you hope to accomplish.

In a moment, we will ask you to write a statement of purpose for your group. To help you do this, we are providing a model statement.

Model Statement of Purpose. This project is designed to provide support group services to a population of individuals who have previously received little or no service—the homebound elderly who are legally blind. These individuals have lost their sight late in life and have had to adapt to this blindness after living their life as sighted persons. The problems they encounter range from losing their right to a drivers license to being unable to tell a $1 bill from a $10 bill. They often live alone. Their loss of vision makes it difficult (if not impossible) for them to get out alone. The purpose of the project would be to implement a method of providing a support group service that would promote the positive capacity of potential members via conference telephoning, a process that has begun to receive extensive use around the country (e.g., see Evans, Smith, Werkhoven, Fox, & Pritzl, 1986; Rittner & Hammons, 1993; Trang & Urbano, 1993). As with all support groups, this service is seen as useful in helping individuals talk about their experiences, share solutions they have discovered, recognize that they are not alone or abnormal in finding their situation painful, receive help, and give help to others in their new role as a visually impaired person, and improve the overall quality of their lives. Telephonic support groups for the elderly blind have been tried elsewhere (e.g., see Evans & Jaureguy, 1981) and have been found to be very effective. The participation of a professionally trained group leader seems necessary for everything from the recruitment of members to managing participation so that everyone has a chance to be active in the group. The purpose of the group would be to increase their reaching out for social contacts (e.g., telephoning or sending tape-recorded letters to family and friends), help increase their feelings of well-being, and enhance their sense of independence.

Before you write your statement, note the following components of a "project purpose" statement:

- A statement of the need for this project—that is, why do it?
- An identification of the target population and a description of their problems—that is, serving who?
- A description of the service to be provided—that is, in what way?
- A brief legitimization for this service as having been used before—that is, method's source?
- A brief description of the role of the professional in providing the service—that is, facilitator's role?
- The organization's purpose for creating this group—that is, purpose?

Now you write similar details about your proposed group and include content that answers these questions:

- Why do it?
- Serving whom?
- In what way?
- Source of this approach?
- Facilitator's role?
- Purpose?

One final admonition: You may be tempted to use shorthand phrases that make sense to you, but because you are practicing the creation of a document that is meant for others who will not know what you know, write your statement out in full in Box 1.1.

Once you have completed your statement, review it in relation to the outline suggested above—that is, Why do it? Serving whom? In what way? Method's source? Worker's role? Purpose? You would probably do well to have a trusted colleague read it as well. Chances are they will see things that need clarification that you have taken for granted.

Box 1.1. Your Statement of Purpose for Your Group

You may have discovered that the discipline imposed by writing this statement has forced you to consider issues you had only thought of in general terms, before you tried to write them out briefly, yet with clarity.

DANGER! In designing this new group work program, you run the risk of creating a group that, from its inception, is designed to focus on the achievement of the *organization's* purposes for creating the group in the first place. New members may recognize or sense that and come to believe that they lack the power to shape their particular group's goals. If you want them to become committed to this group, they must be given ultimate control of the group's goals. The ability to hew to the original purpose of the group, while at the same time helping members to shape its goals, requires skillful and self-disciplined activity on the part of the facilitator. Otherwise, members will not invest in the group.

Next, you will need to consider the costs of this project and where you expect to find the money to fund it.

BUDGETING AND FUNDING

Human service agencies are costly to run, and there are never enough funds to do everything these organizations want to do. Therefore, by definition, any new project (such as the creation of any group) will be viewed by other staff as a competitor for the funds the agency already has allocated to it. The following is a guideline you can apply to this situation: The more you can locate any needed funds from outside of the agency, the more likely you will have the freedom to go forward with your project.

With this guideline in mind, you need to determine the costs your project will entail. Some of these are obvious, and others will be hidden. Obviously, this will cost the agency in terms of your time (which means your salary, that is, the percentage of it you will be devoting to this project). Less obvious are the secretarial services required—for example, recruitment announcements to be typed, duplicated, and mailed out, progress reports to be typed, duplicated, and distributed, and so on. There will also be supplies needed—for example, paper for the secretarial services, telephone costs, refreshments for group meetings, materials consumed by the group in program activities, and so on. Costs will obviously depend on the type of group you plan to run. A telephone support group of the variety used in the model statement of purpose will have much higher telephone bills (for the conference calls) than a group in which the telephone is used primarily to recruit and contact individual members. On the other hand, the telephone group will have zero costs for refreshments because there would be no face-to-face meetings. Some groups go on trips, entailing vehicular costs, whereas others need to rent space because there may be no appropriate space within the agency for certain kinds of group meetings.

Box 1.2 lists some of the types of costs you can anticipate: Fill in the blanks for the projected group for which you wrote the statement of purpose. In some cases, the best you will be able to do is a "ballpark guesstimate."

Box 1.2. Costs You Anticipate for Your Group
for a Defined Period of Time

Staffing: _____

Secretarial: _____

Telephone: _____

Equipment: _____

Program supplies: _____

Rental of space: _____

Refreshments: _____

Other (specify): _____

_____

_____

FUNDING SOURCE

Another guideline: Creation requires creativity.

We have suggested that you would do best to search for outside funding so as not to compete with other staff in your agency for your agency's (always) limited resources.

Question: Which of the following could be true? (Careful: This is a trick question.) (Space for your response is below item C.)

A. You would do best to locate outside funding for your project to avoid competing with others for the agency's resources, thus inviting resistance from your colleagues.

B. If you secure outside funding, you will not need to depend on agency resources, and you will be responsible to the outside funding source: Both of these facts would tend to weaken administrative control of your actions, which administrative staff will not appreciate.

C. If you secure outside funding, administrators will think well of you for generating interest from the outside source because it has the potential for enhancing the agency's status in the community.

Response: A. Yes___ No___   B. Yes___ No___   C. Yes___ No___

In fact, all three could be true—that is, yes, depending on factors such as the agency's current status in the community, the degree of control an outside funding source would expect to exercise over this project, the degree of freedom administrators in your agency are prepared to give you as an innovator, the degree to which this project is your idea or has been stimulated by administrative personnel who have asked you to take it on, and so on. Therefore, the best answer to the question is—it depends on your particular situation.

The number of potential sources for outside funding is actually quite large, including all levels of government, private foundations, local community organizations (ranging from service organizations to churches, etc.), departments within colleges and universities that have a particular interest in your client population, and so on. Probably the best and most widely available source for information on these resources is your local library and the librarian, who can help you find the information you will need. Within the library, you can also find books on how to locate funds: Here we can only point to funding as an essential component of group creation.

ADMINISTRATIVE AND STAFF SUPPORT

Question: Which of the following do you think characterizes most administrators?

A. They want to have an opportunity to personally conduct their agency's program activities.

B. They want to have the ability to predict correctly what their staff will do on their jobs.

Response: (circle one)   A   or   B

If you chose B, you are probably correct. Given the diversity and magnitude of their administrative responsibilities, administrators have neither the time nor the inclination to act as service providers (except, perhaps, in very small agencies or agency units), but they do want to know what their staff is doing and is likely to be doing.

Question: If a new project is to take place, which of the following would most administrators prefer?

A. The project be carried out on a small scale, so it could easily be dropped if it is proving to be a problem.
B. The project be carried out on a grand scale, so the administrator can point to it with pride.

Response: (circle one)   A   or   B

Generally, it is a good idea to do something new on a small scale, without an overly heavy commitment of resources to an unknown venture, so A would be correct. Administrators need to feel that such a project is "reversible" so that they are not stuck with an overcommitment of resources to a project from which it is hard to pull back.

Assume you are a comparatively new staff member. (By "comparatively new," we mean that you have been on staff for less than 6 months.) You have recognized what you see as a serious program deficit that you believe could be resolved by introducing a group work program.

Question: Which of the following is more likely to win administration and staff support?

A. At some point during this comparatively new period, you undertake the creation of a new group. This will let everyone know what a good decision it was to employ you.
B. You should wait until you have been around for at least 6 months before you try to innovate, and during that time do your job (as described in your job description) as well as you can, so that others are impressed with your ability to do the job you were hired to do.

Response: (circle one)   A   or   B

The danger in waiting too long to innovate is that you may become overwhelmed with just doing your job and have no time or inclination to innovate. On the other hand, unless you have demonstrated your ability to do the job you have been assigned to do (in the opinion of your supervisor, at least), other staff will think you are simply trying to show them up and will be less likely to give you the support you will need when you need it. As such, we prefer B.

TARGETS OF THIS NEW GROUP

Given that you are in agreement with all of what has been said previously, you will need to determine whom you are hoping to involve in this group. One way to locate potential members would be to ask staff to refer individuals they know to the pilot group(s) you are planning to create. Unfortunately, practitioners report that this method rarely works unless staff members have decided that this group is needed and have asked you to develop it.

Question: Which of the following approaches do you think will work best? (Some or all of these choices could be correct.)

A. Group members should be recruited from your caseload or people you know personally.

B. Group members should be recruited from another agency in your community—for example, ask a church, hospital, mental health agency, and so on for referrals.

C. Group members should be recruited through public advertising—for example, ads in a local newspaper, and so on.

D. You should ask your supervisor whom you should try to recruit for the group(s).

E. Current or former group members could be asked to recruit members for the group(s).

Response: A___   B___   C___   D___   E___

Actually, any or all of these might work. What is important is that administrators, other staff, and you should have reached a consensus on who should be invited to participate before anyone is invited to participate.

SUMMARY

1. Creating a new group will require a considerable amount of work so that an environment of agency acceptance for the group is developed. By acceptance we mean that administrators, supervisors, and other staff will actively support the innovation you are trying to create.
2. As a first step, you should write a one-page or less statement of purpose that describes why you think this group is needed, whom it would involve, what is known of the method you propose to use in working with this group, how you plan to pay for it, and what the organization's purpose for the group would be.
3. You should plan for a project that is small in scope, so that it can be dropped if it does not achieve its purpose.
4. Before you try to create this new program, you should have been around long enough—about 6 months—to demonstrate to one and all that you are a competent professional.

NEXT

In the next chapter, we take a step backward, in a sense, and try to answer a basic question: Why try to create a group in the first place? To do that, we address some of the following basic questions:

- What is a group?
- What can a group accomplish?
- How do you set the stage for group development to occur?

NOTES

1. We are indebted to our colleague Armand Lauffer and his text (see Lauffer, 1978) for many of the ideas in this chapter, including the notion of an environment of acceptance.

2. By "purpose" we mean the organization's reasons for creating the group. We will be using the word "goals" to refer to the desired outcomes—individual or group or both—selected by group members. The distinction between purpose and goal is discussed later in this book.

2

DEFINING THE TERM GROUP

Before we discuss the process of creating a group, it might be helpful to define what we mean when we use the term *group*. It is a simple enough word, but it represents a complex and much misunderstood concept. Later in this chapter, we will discuss why you would want to create a group in the first place. For now, however, we will deal with the issue of definition.

Question: Given only the information in sentences A and B below, which of the following is likely to be a group and which is probably not?

    A. A line of people at the local Welfare Department.
    B. A meeting of a planning committee at a human service agency.

Response: (circle one)   A   or   B

At first glance, you might be inclined to answer B. Below is a little more information about these two collectivities—that is, collections of people. Perhaps this will lead you to rethink your answer.

    A. The people in the line are all members of a support group for welfare mothers. They are in line to talk with a clerk, to take care of a variety of details pertaining to their grants, before heading off to their regular meeting. They have been meeting once a week for 6 weeks. Each meeting has lasted 1 hour and 30 minutes. The line consists of all of the members of the support group and no one else.
    B. This will be the first meeting of a new planning committee. The committee is composed of seven staff members from the agency's

seven district offices. Because they work in widely scattered offices in this large city, the committee's members scarcely know one another. The committee consists of one representative from each office and a chair from the central office.

Given this information, you might now be more inclined to pick A as the correct answer to the question, "Which of the following is likely to be a group and which is probably not?" After all, the welfare mothers have already met six times, whereas the planning committee has never met.

Actually, there is more to whatever it is that makes a collectivity into a group than the fact that they have or have not met before. Suppose that the welfare mother's group is being led by a staff member who has no training in group facilitation. She has proven to be a very poor group leader. In addition, the women are there as a condition of the grant they are receiving. If asked, each one of the women would tell you that she would prefer to not attend. Meetings are run haphazardly, with no particular purpose articulated for the group, and there are no goals for the group or for the individual members worked out by the group's members. Guest speakers are listened to, politely, but any attempt to introduce discussion of what the guest is presenting (such as how to improve parent-child relationships) goes nowhere.

On the other hand, a great deal of preparation has gone into the agenda for the first meeting of the staff committee. The meeting is chaired by the agency's assistant director. Prior to the meeting, she has contacted each member and built the meeting agenda around their expressed interests. All of the members have volunteered to be on the committee. Members received a thumbnail sketch (from the chair) of each other's background and job responsibilities a week before the meeting. The group was meeting to plan the agency's staff development program for the coming year. They got down to work very quickly and accomplished a great deal in their first meeting.

Now which of these two is a group and which is not? Our answer would be B in the sense that the welfare mothers are simply a collectivity who meet because they must, but that as a collection of people, the nature of their interactions have hardly changed since the first time they met.

Perhaps it will help if we provide the following definition of the word group from Bertcher (1994):

A group is a dynamic social entity composed of two or more individuals. These individuals interact interdependently to achieve one or more common goals for the group, or similar individual goals that each member believes can best be achieved through group participation. As a result of this participation, each member influences and is influenced by every other member to some degree. Over time statuses and roles develop for members, while norms and values that regulate behavior of consequence to the group are accepted by the members. (p. 3)

In one sense, any collection of two or more people could be called a group, but for the purposes of this book, and for your purposes when creating a group, what you hope to achieve is an effective group, which means one that helps participants achieve their individual or group goals, or both, through "interdependent interaction," and one in which, over time, "norms and values" develop that enhance goal achievement. The welfare mothers collectivity, although referred to as a "support group," never actually became a group, whereas the committee was created in such a way that it was an effective group from the start.

Question: Which of the following would you use to measure a group's effectiveness?

    A. Whether or not individual or group goals or both are being achieved.

    B. Whether or not attendance is high.

Response: (circle one)   A   or   B

Because the purpose of creating a group is to achieve particular goals, the correct response is A. If a group goal is to achieve high attendance and if participation is voluntary, however, high attendance could also serve as one indication that the group is being "effective."

By now, you will have guessed that the purpose of this book is to teach you how to create effective groups based on the outcomes achieved by each group participant or by the group as a whole or both.

We have discussed goals. Let's look into that subject by focusing on one group as an example.

Five mothers belong to a support group. Each of them has a son under 10 years of age who has been diagnosed with a terminal disease, cystic fibrosis. The group has been meeting with a facilitator for 4 weeks. During these meetings (which typically run for 1 hour and 30 minutes), they have been discussing how each of them can best cope with her son's illness. During the first meeting, when asked what they hoped to get from this group—that is, to state their individual goals (in terms of what they hoped to be able to do that they could not do now)—they responded with the following answers:

Mrs. A: To be able to answer correctly all of the questions family members and friends continually ask me about my son's illness, both in terms of my satisfaction with my own responses, and their apparent satisfaction with my responses.

Mrs. B: To be able to budget my time so I can give time to my two healthy children and my husband, while still being a good caretaker for my son.

Mrs. C: To be able to meet with and hold on to my child's busy doctor long enough to get straight answers to my questions.

Mrs. D: To keep from feeling so depressed by my son's illness that I am no longer able to function adequately, either at work or at home. Which means, being able to function adequately, at home and at work.

Mrs. E: To be able to help my son manage his illness by following the medical routine prescribed for him, without constant supervision by me.

Question: Have these mothers described individual goals that fit the purpose of this support group?

Response: Yes_____   No_____

The correct answer is yes. The examples show that each has expressed different concerns, but all of them are relevant to the hospital's purpose in establishing a support group for mothers of a child with a terminal illness.

Question: Which of the following could be seen as goals for the group as a whole? (You will find spaces for your response below item D.)

  A. Changing some key hospital procedures that all of the mothers have found unhelpful so that each mother receives the help she seeks.

  B. Planning and carrying out a meeting of the group in which all of the husbands would be present, so that each couple could develop a plan to which both agree about how they should manage their child's illness.

  C. Producing a bimonthly newsletter for distribution to other mothers whose children have been diagnosed with cystic fibrosis.

  D. Creating and maintaining a group in which every member is helped to move toward her individual goals, while each member tries to help the other members move toward their individual goals.

Response: A_____   B_____   C_____   D_____

In fact, all of them are goals of this particular group. When we speak of group goals we are talking about the group as an entity. A clear example of a group goal is the goal of any athletic team to win the game, because it is the goal of the group as an entity to accomplish something. Many treatment, support, and educational groups would not undertake groups goals like A, B, or C (above), but when you think about it, D is a must if a group is to be effective. In fact, for many groups, it is the group's only group goal.

Without an intention to confuse, we present an example from one of our graduate's experience that shows why you (as facilitator) and all of your members have to be clear about your group's goal(s).

A group of welfare mothers had decided that something needed to be done about a city government that had shown itself to be unfriendly to the local welfare program. They had themselves placed on the agenda of city council meetings and spoke there in favor of a more positive approach by the council to a range of matters concerning the welfare program. They had also sought opportunities to have articles published about the accomplishments of the welfare program in the local city newspaper and were currently planning a meeting with their local representative to the state legislature to discuss their concerns about the local program. At the meeting in which they were planning strategy for dealing with the legislator, however, one of the mothers asked for the group's help. Her 14-year-old son had been arrested for dealing drugs, and she did not know how to help him. Members felt torn: The legislator had agreed to meet with them at their next meeting, and they knew they had better be prepared if they wanted to get her attention and support. Members thought that this preparation would take all of the time of their meeting. On the other hand, they knew what this one member was going through regarding her son. Some of them had had similar experiences with their own children.

Question: If you were the facilitator, what would you do? (Please briefly write what you would do.)

_____

_____

_____

_____

_____

You have several options. First and foremost, you could challenge the group to deal with this dilemma of group needs versus individual needs. Empowering members to seek third alternatives is one of the most useful approaches a facilitator can help the group to experience. If the group asks for your suggestions, you might suggest that the group schedule an extra meeting to discuss this mother's immediate problem, or you might suggest that she meet, as an individual, with an agency staff member who has had experience dealing with the court. You might even suggest to the group that this was an example of the kind of problems that welfare parents experience and build her situation into the presentation to the legislator. Our point is that this mother's individual need (and her goal to protect her son, while correcting his behavior) really did not fit the group's goal of affecting city government's approach to the welfare program. As such, it created a conflict of priorities for the group as it tried to achieve its goals, but it also offered a wonderful conflict resolution opportunity for the group.

SUMMARY

The term group refers to a collection of people who interact to help one another achieve some goal or goals. These goals can pertain to what the group, as an entity, hopes to achieve, or they can pertain to each member's hopes for himself or herself. In a relatively brief amount of time, a collection of individuals can develop into an effective group as they move toward individual or group goal achievement or both, and in their development, to create norms and values to regulate the way they interact. Your task is to facilitate this process of group development by "structuring the group in a fashion that facilitates each patient's autonomous functioning" (Yalom, 1983, p. 125).

P.S.:
WHY CREATE A GROUP?

Question: We create a group because

- A. It is nice to socialize with other people.
- B. People can help one another to achieve their individual or group goals, or both, better through group participation than they can by themselves.

Response: (circle one)   A   or   B

Socializing can be nice, but the fact is, achieving one's goals through a group is more important. Experience and research both attest to the effectiveness of group efforts in solving problems. For example, Toseland and Siporin's (1986) wide-ranging study of group treatment found that

- Individual help is never more effective nor efficient than group help.
- Group help is sometimes more effective and efficient than individual help.
- The dropout rate is much higher for individual help than for group help.

Question: The following is a list of areas in which a group might be helpful. Rate each item in relation to the following scale by filling in the blanks with what you consider to be the appropriate letter from the rating scale.

A = always true
B = usually true
C = sometimes true
D = rarely true
E = never true

A group can

1. _____ Generate more ideas about ways to achieve a goal than any one individual can.
2. _____ Provide a variety of role models from whom to learn new skills.
3. _____ Help an individual to recognize that one's reactions to difficulty are not abnormal.
4. _____ Provide supportive social relationships to lonely, isolated individuals.
5. _____ Provide an opportunity for individuals with a negative self-image to see themselves in a positive light when they are helpful to others.
6. _____ Provide an opportunity for an individual to be in total control of other people.
7. _____ Provide an opportunity for members of oppressed populations to become empowered and move out of the role of "victim."
8. _____ Create an environment in which an individual can practice new ways of thinking and acting with supportive feedback from peers.
9. _____ Confront an individual with group norms and pressures to require him or her to consider new (for them) values.
10. _____ Provide an opportunity to have fun during social interaction without that "fun" harming anyone.

11. _____ Provide an opportunity for members to help other people who are faced with similar difficulties to the ones they are facing.

12. _____ Achieve some outcome, as a group, that none of them could achieve alone.

With the exception of Item 6 about total control of other people (which should have been rated E), we think you should have rated all the other items an A or a B. We think that is a pretty impressive list of reasons for engaging in group creation.

NEXT

In our next chapter, we describe the different kinds of groups with which you may be working and the ways in which these differences affect the process of group creation.

3

DIFFERENT KINDS OF GROUPS

Because there are many ways to categorize groups, we will describe ours and ask you to use it as you read through this book. (See Bertcher, 1994, pp. 180-185, for a more complete discussion of group types.)

1. *Treatment groups* are therapeutic groups designed to help individuals work toward changing significant psychosocial problems they face that involve their self-concept or their social relationships or both so that each member can function as a competent human being who is achieving his or her own goals. Leadership of such groups is usually performed by trained human service professionals.

2. *Support groups* are designed to help individuals who are struggling to cope with the same kind of problem by seeking and giving support to one another. Emphasis is on management of a common illness—for example, hemophilia, alcoholism, and so on—or a common role—for example, caretaking. Leadership of such groups may be carried out by persons with the illness itself or with that "common role" (and these are people who lack formal training in a human service profession), by human service professionals, or by a mix of the two.

3. *Educational groups* include continuing education classes, Headstart classes, agency training groups, graduate school courses, and so on that are designed to impart knowledge, teach skills, or consider value issues or all three. These groups make no assumption (as do the first two group types) that members are experiencing personal difficulties in their lives. It is expected, however, that members will use their learning to move to a more competent level of autonomous functioning. Leadership is provided by persons with a range of professional preparation for their role as "teacher." Although the facilitator may play an active role in recruiting members for such a group, he or she often has very little to say about who shows up for such a group.

4. In contrast to these three types of groups, *task groups* exist to achieve some group outcome with no particular focus on the individual change of its members, as is the case with the first three groups. Leadership may be the result of an electoral process—for example, a committee's chairperson—or may be associated with the leader's employment position—for example, an agency director. In some task groups, the facilitator is not the group's formal leader—for example, an agency board of directors has a chair, and the agency's executive director acts as the group's facilitator. Occasionally, treatment groups and support groups take on some group goal, often in relationship to a social action project, and become—for a time—a task group. Fatout and Rose's (1995) book on task groups should prove helpful in an examination of issues in the creation of task groups.

5. *Residential groups* are for individuals who live together in prisons, hospitals, summer camps, and so on. As part of their 24-hour-a-day interaction, these individuals may be involved in any of the four group types defined previously.

6. *Groups on the Internet.* Although these groups are not discussed further in this book, we would be failing you, the reader, if we did not call attention to this computer-bred innovation, for it has had an astonishing growth in a very short period of time. Computer bulletin boards, news groups, and other formats all offer people the opportunity to communicate (via computer and modem) in relation to an unlimited number of subjects, some dealing with human service issues. For example, a colleague's daughter was about to adopt a baby, so he "joined" a group on the Internet in which issues associated with adoption were discussed. In short order, he found himself in communication with people all over the world who wrote messages to everyone in the group about adoption. Participants then responded to these messages if they wished to do so, and of course, he occasionally wished to do so. He found these message exchanges very thought provoking and useful. Participants in these groups often disguise their true identities and, given the protection of anonymity, are able to reveal very private concerns. For example, in a recent issue of *Time* magazine devoted completely to "Cyberspace," a participant in one of these groups wrote, " 'I told him things I had never told anyone. He was able to be more open too' " ("Cyberspace," 1995, p. 24). Apparently, anonymity is very liberating and helps people to communicate freely. In some ways, this is similar to the openness of communication that people experience in group work by telephone but has the added characteristic of time delay in responding, giving participants time to consider the message they want to send. (Unlike a face-to-face group, in which the courtesy of a more or less immediate response is expected, these groups eliminate time as a response factor.)

To create such a group, one merely needs to sign on to the Internet using a piece of software that makes it possible to connect with the Internet. At the University of Michigan, for example, a faculty member can create a group consisting of the members of his or her class. Some groups can be joined as one "surfs" (inspects) the Internet, whereas others are non-joinable. A group can have a moderator in which all messages go through the moderator. This individual controls the flow of communication by deciding which messages to pass on to the group. The varieties are too numerous to describe here but can become clear to the interested reader who is able to consult any source of information about the Internet.[1] These days, that means almost any university. At the University of Michigan, for example, consultation is available from its Information Technology Division.

The roles of the facilitator and participants in this "group" are so different from those in the group types described previously that we will not refer to this group type again. Nevertheless, these groups have an amazing potential for helping participants with major life problems.[2] One can imagine a social worker referring a group member to a particular group on the Internet to find some new perspectives (in relation to a problem) that he or she has not been able to locate within his or her treatment group. We believe that the use of electronic groups will be expanding rapidly in the future, and therefore we could not ignore their existence.

Question: Which one of the following do you think is the most important consideration in planning for the creation of all of the six group types? (Respond below item E.)

    A. Financial support for the group's work.
    B. What the group is established to achieve—that is, its purpose.
    C. The availability of potential members.
    D. An appropriate meeting facility.
    E. An environment of acceptance for the creation of the group.

Response: (circle one)   A   B   C   D   E

From what you have read so far, you might be inclined to respond that all five are of critical importance when planning a group's creation—and they are—but as you read on, you will find that our primary emphasis will always be on B, what the group is established to achieve—that is, its purpose.

The following are our reasons for saying that every major decision concerning a group's creation eventually depends on the purpose of the group.

    A. Financial support: The justification for expending money for any group is the purpose(s) for which it is being created. If the purpose is accepted as important, then it is worth spending funds to achieve it.

B. Member availability: The kinds of people you recruit for the group depend on the purpose of the group.

C. Meeting facility: The facility you will require depends on the kind of group you want to create. A 7-member treatment group needs a very different kind of facility than a 21-member committee. Again, facility requirements are based on the purpose of the group.

D. The environment of acceptance: The environment of acceptance discussed in Chapter 1 includes an agreement among key staff that this new group is needed to achieve a particular purpose or set of purposes.

Group purpose is therefore viewed in this text as the critical factor in a range of factors pertaining to group creation.

One further point: We have deliberately chosen the word purpose rather than the word goal to emphasize the point that some individual or organization creates the group to achieve a particular purpose, but that once the group is created, its members should select the goals for this particular group. By giving the members the right to select their own goals, we empower them in a way that will increase their loyalty to their group. This loyalty will, we believe, facilitate the group's development, which is critical if the group is to be effective—that is, achieve the purpose for which it was created in the first place. Let's see how clear this point is.

Question: Which of the following is likely to be a group's purpose (P) and which is likely to be a group's goal (G)?

A. To change an agency policy that members consider an obstacle to achieving their goals. (circle one) P or G

B. To provide service to a previously unreached population the agency should be serving. P or G

C. To challenge students to reconsider their values concerning controversial issues in a profession. P or G

D. To create a prison newspaper that will serve as a forum for the views of both prison officials and prisoners. P or G

E. To help caretakers of persons diagnosed with Alzheimer's disease to provide the best care possible. P or G

F. To acquire the most recent and accurate information about residential care facilities for individuals diagnosed with Alzheimer's disease. P or G

G. To create an atmosphere of support for group members' attempts to learn how to "fight fair" in marriage, so that each partner's life is enriched. P or G

In our opinion (referring to your responses above):

A. This is a goal that probably grew out of a discussion in which members discovered a common negative reaction to an agency policy and decided to do something about it—that is, create a new group goal.

B. This is a purpose devised by an agency's staff to fulfill its community mandate.

C. This is a purpose of a teacher in designing a new course.

D. This one is tricky: A group for residents could decide it can hold its members' interests best if it becomes—for at least part of its time together—a task group running a newspaper. This would be a group goal that evolved out of their interactions. On the other hand, a staff member may have thought a newspaper would recruit interested members, whereas a talk group (such as the kind they had tried in the past with little success) would not. The selection of this purpose by staff is not initially a group's goal for itself, but in time, members would likely create their own goals for the newspaper. You would need more information before you could determine whether this is a purpose or a goal.

E. This is the purpose of the local Alzheimer's Association in creating a support group.

F. This is one goal of a particular support group that was created by the Alzheimer's Association. Notice that the goals a group selects for itself are often in harmony with the organization's purpose for creating the group, but whether they are or are not, they should be focused on the specific needs and interests of the particular individuals who comprise the group if the members are to experience their group as being effective.

G. This is likely the goal of a specific treatment group in which members have talked about the fact that several of them are experiencing difficulty with the particular issue of managing conflict in their marriage.

THE ROLE OF THE FACILITATOR
IN DIFFERENT KINDS OF GROUPS

A graduate student in her field placement was observed to be immobilized by the treatment group to which she had been assigned. When asked why, she said, "I want to be sure I'm doing everything 'by the book' " (by which she meant in the exactly correct way). Her mentor, a social worker in the agency who was serving as her field instructor, laughed and replied, "Which book?" Indeed, there are many ways to conduct treatment groups, as discussed, for example, in Shaffer and Galinsky's (1989) *Models of Group Therapy.* For each of these approaches, the role of the facilitator ("therapist" is the term used by many for this role but not by all) is somewhat different. Accordingly, in writing about the role of the facilitator in relation to the first four kinds of groups described previously, we prefer to compare the facilitator's role in the four kinds of groups by comparing certain factors that characterize each kind of role and help to determine the nature of the facilitator's role in each. These factors are (a) attendance, (b) frequency of meeting, (c) size, and (d) expectations about participation.

Question: How do you think the facilitator's role in each of the group types is affected with regard to member attendance only?

Treatment: _____

_____

Support: _____

_____

Educational: _____

_____

Task: _____

_____

The following is how we believe the facilitator's role is affected with regard to attendance.

Treatment Groups. Attendance in many treatment groups is voluntary, although in residential programs attendance is often involuntary. For those groups in which attendance is voluntary, the expectation is that members will not miss a session. If they do, they will be confronted with the observation that they are resisting the treatment process. If members fail to attend regularly, they may be dropped from the group. For the facilitator, this means that he or she will be the person confronting the member who fails to attend on a regular basis.

Support Groups. It is expected that attendance will be irregular. The support group facilitator might prefer regularity of attendance from everyone but does not require it or in any way confront the irregularly attending member. In fact, it is often the case that members attend sporadically making it difficult for the facilitator to develop a sense of "groupness" among the members.

Educational Groups. Depending on the nature of the sponsoring organization, members who fail to attend may or may not face serious consequences. In our school, for example, we are expected to inform the advisor of students who miss three classes in a row, and a student's grade may be negatively impacted by poor attendance. This puts the facilitator-teacher in the role of monitor and "punisher" with regard to attendance.

Task Groups. Facilitators always hope for 100% attendance but take no immediate action when a member misses a meeting. Many task groups are representative of various constituencies, however, so that a member's absence can mean that that constituency is not represented when important decisions are being made by the group. If a member fails to attend regularly, the facilitator may ask him or her to find another person from his or her constituency who could attend regularly, or contact the constituency itself, and ask for a different representative.

Question: How do you think the facilitator's role is affected with regard to a group's frequency of meeting only?

Treatment: _____

_____

Support: _____

_____

Educational: _____

_____

*Task:*_____

_____

Treatment Groups. Many treatment groups meet once a week, although in residential settings, treatment groups may meet once a day, 5 days a week, with time off on the weekends, when facilitators are recovering from their weeklong duties. The once-a-week groups allow the facilitator time to review last week's group meeting and plan for next week's, to contact colleagues about individual members, and to carry out collateral activities on behalf of group members.

Support Groups. Some support groups meet once or twice a month, which makes it difficult for the facilitator to assure continuity from one meeting to the next. This problem is compounded by the irregularity of attendance mentioned previously. As a result, the support group facilitator has to be continually ready to shift focus and alter planning to fit the particular constellation of individuals who attend any one meeting.

Educational Groups. Depending on the setting, educational groups may meet with a predictable time frame. Headstart classes would meet daily, graduate school classes might meet once a week, and staff training sessions might meet once a month. The greater the time between meetings, the more time the facilitator has to reflect on the past meeting and plan for the next meeting. In educational groups, it is often the case that the group members seek out the facilitator for further instruction on an individual level. Facilitators often find that they do some of their best teaching away from the group, when they fit their teaching activities to the individual needs of that one student.

Task Groups. The frequency with which task groups meet depends on the nature of the task they have undertaken. A board of directors might meet once a month to carry out routine business, whereas a community action group, involved in a strike, might meet daily or even more often, to plot strategy or decide how to respond to an unexpected move from its opponents. In either case (and we have presented extremes to make the point) the role of the facilitator in all types of groups will be shaped by the frequency of the group's meetings.

Question: How do you think the facilitator's role is affected with regard to group size only?

Treatment: _____

_____

Support: _____

_____

Educational: _____

_____

Task: _____

_____

Treatment Groups. Most treatment groups are comparatively small: four to nine members. Anything larger, most therapists would say, would seriously impede the ability to attend to the needs of individual members. The small size (when compared to the other kinds of groups) does not make the facilitator's role easier because the problems being dealt with are complex and require more individualized attention than is the case (again, therapists would say) in the other three kinds of groups.

Support Groups. A support group leader was quoted as saying, "On some nights we have 5 members show up, on other nights, 25. We never know ahead of time how many people will show." This wide variation in size, and the inability to predict the regular presence of even a core group, makes the support group facilitator's job different from the treatment group facilitator's, where attendance is pretty regular and the group has a chance to grow and develop. In this sense, the support group facilitator has to be very flexible with regard to maintaining among members the idea that this is a group rather than a happenstance collection of people who show up at the same place at the same time.

Educational Groups. In many cases, budget realities require educational groups to be large—for example, 30—so that attention to individual needs is more difficult for the facilitator. Given the fact that facilitators of educational groups often have little to do with group composition, this may be the group (of the four types) that is most difficult to develop as a group. Indeed, many facilitators of educational groups are little concerned about the group's development and more intent on achieving individual growth with regard to the instructional content being delivered.

Task Groups. The ideal size for a task group often depends on the complexity of the tasks it undertakes. Size may also be dictated by political realities: If the group is to be representative of various constituencies, the number of constituencies and the number of representatives required from each constituency may determine the group's size. In some cases, a large group may prove unwieldy and, based on experience, a facilitator may try to keep the group small—for example, five members—to ensure task completion.

Question: How do you think the facilitator's role is affected with regard to the expected participation level of each member only?

Treatment: _____

_____

Support: _____

_____

Educational: _____

_____

Task: _____

_____

Treatment Groups. Given the wide array of treatment models, the major participant in a group may be the facilitator, who is viewed as the prime source of help and the person through whom most communication flows. Often, a meeting focuses on one individual, and participation of other members focuses—for that meeting—on the needs of that member. Eventually, all members are expected to be the focus of the group's attention with significant attention to the achievement of individualized treatment goals. When someone is the focal person, he or she is expected to respond openly and honestly, and the facilitator is expected to help him or her do so.

Support Groups. Participation may be of the round-robin variety, in which every person in the group's seating circle is expected to share his or her current concerns in one meeting, and all members are expected to provide support and guidance to the person currently reporting to the group. The facilitator is expected to keep the ball rolling, so that everyone has a chance to be heard, and to encourage members to help one another. In a support group, the facilitator is supposed to be just that—a facilitator of participation—but the prime source of helpfulness is meant to be the members themselves, so they are expected to interact helpfully.

Education Groups. Some facilitators prefer to lecture in an uninterrupted fashion. In such a situation, members are not expected to participate verbally unless they wish to ask questions.

Other facilitators prefer an instructional situation in which members interact to a high degree often in small subgroups. Here, the facilitator is likely to play the role of consultant to the subgroups, responding to requests or, when there are no requests, visiting subgroups to ensure that they are making progress. Still other facilitators prefer an interactive teaching mode, where the interaction is with the group as a whole. Forming subgroups is an act of group creation, albeit the facilitator cannot have interaction with each subgroup at the same time. Interacting with the class as a whole (given the comparatively large size of many classes) makes it difficult to create a sense of belonging to a group for all members.

Task Groups. Members are all expected to participate actively, albeit each may be expected to identify their particular area of expertise or interest in some component of the larger task and participate primarily in that area. It is therefore not uncommon for the group to operate—at times—in subgroups, and—at times—as a total group. When this happens, the facilitator may play an active role in deciding who will be in what subgroup, and in this way, try to use group creation to move the group forward.

In discussing the role of facilitators in the four types of groups, we have tried—sometimes directly and sometimes indirectly—to suggest how facilitators in each kind of group can use group creation to support group development processes.

SUMMARY

A group's purpose(s) is directly related to the type of group it is (treatment, support, educational, task, residential, or electronic) and the factors that led to its creation, whereas a group's goal(s) grows out of its members' interests, needs, and concerns, once the group has begun to meet. Both purpose and goal pertain to outcomes or results, or both, and are critical concepts in our discussion of group creation.

NOTES

1. See, for example, "Online Directory Services—X-500 User Overview," University of Michigan, Information Technology Division (1994). This handout provides specific information about how to create different kinds of groups as well as how to find and join a group.

2. For example, see Finn and Lavitt (1994). This article's extensive four-page bibliography provides a fine review of the currently relevant literature.

4

RECRUITING GROUP MEMBERS

All groups need members. Some groups, by their nature—that is, with regard to their purpose—do not need many members—for example, 5 could be about right for some treatment groups. Some—again in terms of purpose—need a lot of members—for example, 25 could be about right for some task groups. Whatever the desired size, however, you need a way to recruit people who are "right" for the particular group you are trying to create and right in sufficient numbers so that you can select (from that pool of potential members) the best possible mix for this particular group. (Mix is discussed further in Chapter 5. For now, our focus is on recruiting potential members for any kind of group.)

Actually, there are two types of recruitment.

1. *Direct recruitment:* This involves personal contact by the facilitator—that is, the person creating the group—with potential group members.
2. *Indirect recruitment:* In this approach, the facilitator contacts various referral agents and asks them to identify potential members.

In some situations—for example, a high school—there are so many potential members for such a wide variety of groups (again, in terms of purpose) that identifying potential members for a particular group is not very difficult. In other situations, finding anyone interested in joining your proposed group may be the most difficult step in group creation.

Recruitment of referral agents is similar to direct recruitment: You would want to provide them with a statement of purpose—a purpose that clearly meets the needs of people with whom they deal.

Question: Think about any group you might join. What might cause you to hesitate to join it?

Response: _____

_____

_____

_____

See how your list compares with ours. Our list pertains to anyone being asked to join any kind of group.

1. Many people have had bad experiences in some group, somewhere, sometime. If you investigate, you will learn that the reason they had their bad experience may have been because the group lacked a competent facilitator to protect everyone from a negative experience; that does not matter to your potential recruit. What they remember is being embarrassed, drawn into unpleasant struggles over power, experiencing defeat as part of a group that tried to accomplish some task, and so on. Sometimes, even though a group facilitator was present, he or she may have lacked the skill to facilitate widespread participation, so that the group fell into a pattern of high participation by a few members and almost no participation by most. Given all of these difficulties, it is not surprising that some potential members are gun-shy about getting into a group where they can be hurt, ignored, or disappointed again.

2. Treatment and support groups require each member to talk about private matters: People are often uncomfortable about sharing such information with others. That fact alone is enough to scare away many people, particularly if they have never experienced the benefits of such sharing.

3. It is unfortunately the case that many people act in the role of group facilitator (or chairperson, teacher, coordinator, etc.) without appropriate training or skill to perform their role effectively. Potential members might want to avoid a group in which they lack confidence in the announced leader(s).

4. We have all gone through class groups where our primary goal became pass the (blankety-blank) course; we have survived in-service training that was required but irrelevant to our needs. Therefore, it is not surprising that some people are gun-shy when joining an educational group.

5. Task groups that got waylaid by internal bickering, hurt feelings, dominating subgroups, or ineffective leadership encourage individuals to go it alone when there is a task to be done.

6. Sometimes group participation is required—for example, as a condition of probation that was ordered by a court or in terms of an assignment to a committee that looks as if it will be a time waster. In those situations, it is

understandable that potential members would want to avoid an involuntary assignment to a group.

7. Attending a group may be one responsibility too many for a person already overburdened with responsibilities—for example, a mother of a child with cancer who is involved in all sorts of caretaking activities for her child, while at the same time trying to fulfill her roles as wife and mother to healthy children, or a potential task group member who already has a "full plate" of responsibilities and does not want to join one more committee.

In other words, there are many ways groups can be perceived as unpleasant, boring, an unneeded burden, or even frightening for some. Anyone who goes recruiting had better know that and be prepared to counteract the negative reputation groups have acquired. Of course, many people have had positive experiences in groups (and these people can be a wonderful resource as a group member) but never forget that many have not. This suggests that it would be wise, when trying to recruit an individual, to ask about the kinds of group experiences the individual has had, and when he or she describes how they have been negative, explain how this one will be different. In addition, look for a few people who can tell positive stories about past group experiences.

Question: The following is a list of recruitment conditions. Think about a group that you might be invited to join. Put a "Y" (for yes) next to the conditions that would lead you to think favorably about joining that group, an "N" (for no) for those that would not work for you, and a "U" (for undecided) where you would not be sure that you wanted to join and would want more information before you would decide on a yes response. After you have finished this list, we will tell you how we would rate each recruiting condition and why.

A. ____ Membership in this group is entirely voluntary.

B. ____ The purpose of this group fits with a current interest of yours.

C. ____ The plan for this group is to meet at a time that would be difficult for you to make.

D. ____ All of the other members will be strangers.

E. ____ The operation of the group will be left entirely to the people who comprise it.

F. ____ Free refreshments will be a regular part of the group meeting.

G. ____ At least one of the other members will be someone you know and like.

H. ____ The group will meet for a limited period of time—for example, eight weekly meetings.

I. ____ Within the general purpose of the group, members will be able to determine particular goals for their group or for themselves or both.

J. ____ The group will include people with a variety of viewpoints.

Now add, if you wish, three other conditions that would attract you to the idea of joining this group.

K. _____

L. _____

M. _____

What are three other conditions that would lead you to want to

avoid this group?

N. _____

O. _____

P. _____

In one sense, there are no right or wrong answers because your answers reflect your own prior experience with group membership. We have some notions about what would make a group attractive, however, when you are trying to market the idea of joining any group. Therefore, the following is our thinking about each of the conditions.

A. We prefer empowering individuals, and one way to do this is to give them control over the decision to join or not to join any group you are trying to create. As such, our choice would be Y.

B. Generally, people prefer to become part of something that they can see will benefit them. Again, our choice is Y.

C. We prefer to not place impediments in the way of group participation. Scheduling a group at a bad time for a particular population of potential members would not help recruitment. N.

D. Some groups deal with personal issues in which it is important for members to know that what they say will not be circulated among friends and family. Therefore, although it may not be too easy to deal with strangers initially, that may actually be a "plus" (knowing that what goes on in the group will remain in the group—that is, because none of the other members are acquaintances or family, it is highly unlikely that what goes on in the group will be reported back to other acquaintances or family). In addition, starting with a group of strangers allows one to start fresh, with one's prior reputation unknown, and that could also be a plus. Therefore, although this appears, at first glance, to be a poor recruitment strategy, it may actually be a good way to begin. We vote Y. Did you vote as we did?

E. This sounds too unstructured to us, leaving the way open to many of the tragedies that people have known in earlier group experiences. N.

F. Free eats! Great! Y.

G. It depends on the group. Given what we said previously in response to D, we would leave this as a U and look at other factors about any particular group.

H. Requiring a limited commitment seems likely to be less demanding—at this point in time. In some cases, members might decide to extend the life of the group, once they have begun to meet, but then it would be their decision. Y.

I. Letting potential members know that they will have much to say about the specific issues the group will address is a further way of empowering them and seems likely to attract potential members. Y.

J. For some, this might make the group more attractive. Others might anticipate too much conflict. This one is hard to tell without knowing more about the group. U.

THE SALESPITCH

A FREE SAMPLE

Have you ever taken a child of yours for orthodontia? One of us did, when our daughter was 12. Daughter and dad were led to a small room, in which we watched a 12-minute film that graphically portrayed the process she would be going through. This was very helpful in terms of knowing what to expect. (Unfortunately, the film was of no use in helping us figure out how to pay for the work. Nevertheless, we thought it helped us understand the necessity of buying this service.) Salespeople know full well the value of providing samples of their wares, and there is much to be learned from that.

Question: Which of the following approaches would be feasible for you when trying to recruit potential group members?

A. ____ Showing them a videotape (or playing an audiotape) of a portion of a group meeting—a group like the one they are being invited to join. (This assumes you have permission from all of the members of the group you taped to use such a tape for this purpose.)

B. ____ Inviting potential members to visit (as a nonparticipating observer) a group meeting. (Again, this assumes that members of the group being observed give permission for an observer to be present.)

C. ____ Showing a potential member a portion of a script of a group meeting of the kind of group they are being invited to join. (Here the identities of all members would be disguised and, again, their permission to show such a script would be required.)

D. ____ Given that none of the above are available, meeting with the potential member, prior to a group meeting, and describing the way in which the group tends to operate using specific examples from recent meetings of groups that are similar to the one being formed.

We hope that at least one of these is feasible for you.

GROUP MEMBERS AS RECRUITERS

For some groups, individuals who have already agreed to be members might be willing to actively recruit other individuals who they believe could benefit from or make a good contribution to the group or both. For example, one practitioner we spoke to reported starting his treatment groups in a school with four children referred by teachers. He would describe the purpose of the group in general terms, then ask each member to bring a friend to the next meeting—a friend who could use a group like this. He reported that the groups he created in this way tended to be effective.

GROUP MEMBERS CHOOSING
THEIR OWN FACILITATORS

In situations in which potential members know potential facilitators, allowing a treatment or support group to recruit its own facilitator recognizes their investment in the group. Thus a staff member may be the creator of a group but, eventually, not its facilitator. In such groups, members might also invite single-session facilitators to meet specific needs of the group. In task groups, it is often the case that members choose their own "leader" from among the group, as when they elect a committee chair. As noted previously, this chair may not be the group's facilitator if the group is led by a staff member of the group's sponsoring organization.

PUBLICITY

Often, the problem with creating a new group is letting potential members know that there is a plan to create such a group. One practitioner reported posting ads in her city's public buses—a group for men who were battering their wives and wanted to stop. She reported an active telephone response to this ad and was able to recruit all of the members she needed.

Where such publicity is posted depends on the purpose of the group and assumptions you will make about where potential group members are most likely to see or hear about the group. Different populations will respond to different "pitches," but brief descriptions of the planned-for group might do well to highlight some of the conditions described previously—for example, a university's counseling service might place the following ad in the student newspaper:

> GRIEVING OVER A LOST LOVE RELATIONSHIP? The University's Counseling Services is planning a support group designed to help individuals cope with overwhelming feelings of grief that are interfering with their life. The group will be free, will consist of 6 to 8 female student members, will meet for 8 weeks, and will ensure confidentiality for all participants. If you are interested, call Gloria Bee, Social Worker, at 123-4567 for more information.

SUMMARY

Finding potential members is a critical step in group creation. The circumstances in which this search takes place vary widely depending on the setting in which the group will operate and the organization's purpose for creating the group. Typically, creating a group requires an active recruiting process and, as with any recruitment effort, a fair amount of salesmanship is involved. It is often the case that you would like this recruitment to create more than enough potential members so attention can be given to creating the best mix of people for any particular group. In Chapter 5, we will discuss the issues involved in composing a group once (and if) you have a pool of potential members lined up and interested in group membership.

It is also important to provide some other opportunities to potential members who have been contacted, invited to consider joining a particular group, and then—in effect—"rejected" as being inappropriate for a particular group. For example, persons recruited for a treatment group or a support group, and then found to be inappropriate for this group, should be referred to some other form of service such as one-to-one counseling, couple therapy, family treatment, or even a different group. Individuals recruited for a task group may turn out to not be needed or may be wrong for this particular group. With a task group, you might do well to be selective when you recruit to avoid "leftovers."

One special problem you may have with a task group that is meant to include representatives of various constituencies is that you have almost no control over who shows up for your first group meeting. If you see that this is your reality, you can ask the organizations or groups that send representatives to select individuals who meet particular criteria, such as experience with the issues your group will be addressing, the degree to which they actually represent the thinking of the constituency they are representing, or demonstrated ability to be an active participant in group deliberations, and so on.

In cases of indirect recruitment, the person referred to the group will be unaware of the fact that he or she has not been accepted for a particular group, so it should be unnecessary to provide alternative opportunities.

5

COMPOSING YOUR GROUP

Having identified a number of potential members, we now must decide which mix of these individuals has the best potential for becoming an effective group. In preparing to write this second edition, we interviewed a number of practitioners and graduate students in field training about their experiences with group creation. Many of them informed us that they have little control over group composition and have to settle for whoever shows up. That is a reality in practice that we can respect. We think, however, there are certain guidelines, which we present below, that will help you to think about and use group composition as an influencing factor in facilitating group development and group effectiveness. We encourage you to seek as much control over group composition as you can achieve. We begin this process by attending to the attributes of potential members.

An attribute is any characteristic or quality by which an individual may be described or compared with others or both.

Question: Of the two sets of attributes below, which is specific and which is nonspecific?

    A. Happy, sloppy, unreliable
    B. Age, gender, marital status

Response: Specific _____   Nonspecific _____

Obviously, the specific set of attributes is B, primarily because we can measure such attributes with precision. In creating a group, we try to determine the specific attributes that describe potential members and then attempt to assemble a group of individuals with a particular mix of attributes. To do this, we describe each potential member in terms of the following two kinds of attributes:

1. Descriptive attributes that can be used to classify an individual—for example, married, unemployed, resident of Michigan, and so on
2. Behavioral attributes that describe the way an individual has acted in the past and therefore is likely to act in the future—for example, ability to verbalize feelings, capacity to solve complex human problems, ability to deal with pressure, and so on

It should be possible to be specific when describing an individual in terms of descriptive attributes, but it is harder to be specific regarding behavioral attributes because more subjective judgment is involved in the description of someone's patterns of behavior. Therefore, we recommend that you pay attention to an individual's self-reported behavioral patterns. Unless you have had an opportunity to observe them in action, or to talk with someone who has—for example, a teacher, family member, workmate, and so on—self-report is often the only way to describe a person's behavioral attributes. Because these self-reports may be inaccurate or incomplete, some facilitators have created one-session groups for the purpose of describing and discussing what the group will be like (which is one way to provide a sample of the group that was discussed in Chapter 4), while at the same time observing the behavioral attributes of potential group members.

Question: Which of the following attributes is descriptive (D) and which is behavioral (B)?

1. Is 25 years old. B_____ D_____
2. Refuses to play with other children. B_____ D_____
3. Is a former psychiatric hospital patient. B_____ D_____
4. Has been known to be very talkative in social situations. B_____ D_____
5. Has run away from home. B_____ D_____
6. Is African American. B_____ D_____

In responding to this question, you probably wrote that 1, 3, and 6 were descriptive attributes because they referred to categories or classifications of people, whereas 2 and 4 were behavioral attributes because they referred to someone's actions. Number 5 might have puzzled you a bit because it seems to refer to an action, but in fact it is simply another way of categorizing this individual. Running away from situations may or may not be a pattern of behavior—that is, the way the person is likely to behave in the future—but it is clearly a classification of this individual (a descriptive attribute).

Attributes should be stated as clearly as possible. For example, "This person is a member of the Detroit Lions football team" classifies him—that is, refers to a descriptive attribute—whereas "This person plays football for the Lions in a ferocious manner" describes his actions—that is, refers to a behavioral attribute. Less clear (as a description of an individual's attributes) would be "This person plays football for the Detroit Lions" because it could refer to his classification as a member of the team (descriptive) or to his ability to play football at a professional level (behavioral).

Moral: When describing someone's attributes, be as specific as you can!

One further point about attributes before we show you how to use them when composing a group. Every individual can be described in terms of dozens of attributes. Which would you use to help you determine who would be appropriate for any particular group? To deal with this question, we invented the notion of the *critical attribute*—that is, those few attributes that you would use when composing a group. How do you decide which attributes are critical? You look at the group's purpose and select those particular attributes that pertain most directly to that purpose.

Question: Given the plan of the university's counseling services to create a group for the purpose of helping female students cope more effectively with recently lost relationships, what are three critical descriptive attributes that should characterize each potential member of this group?

Critical descriptive attribute 1: _____

Critical descriptive attribute 2: _____

Critical descriptive attribute 3: _____

How about critical behavioral attributes?

Critical behavioral attribute 1: _____

Critical behavioral attribute 2: _____

Critical behavioral attribute 3: _____

Selecting the three critical descriptive attributes should be fairly self-evident.

- Female
- Registered as a student at the university
- Person who reports that they have recently lost an important relationship

Selecting critical behavioral attributes is more difficult and often involves a creative imagination. We would include the following:

- The ability to describe how they have managed their feelings so that they could deal with their daily lives
- Their performance as students (because a loss can sometimes interfere with a person's ability to perform his or her student role satisfactorily)
- Their ability to problem solve life issues independently (because eventually each will have to cope with his or her loss in a way that allows him or her to get on with life)

The following is our guideline regarding the use of attributes when composing a group, based on the experience of practitioners (and what we have been building up to in this chapter): The most effective groups are those in which the members are similar with regard to critical descriptive attributes and mixed with regard to critical behavioral attributes.

Having set forth this "rule," let us explain (a) what supports it and (b) when to ignore it! We will use the group for women who have recently lost a relationship, mentioned previously, as our example.

In regard to the critical descriptive attributes listed previously:

- *Female:* Although the loss of a relationship is difficult for both men and women, it is likely that gender will play a role in how someone reacts to that loss. People of the same gender are likely to have some immediate affinity for others who have experienced a loss—an affinity that will help them to communicate in a way that should facilitate group development. Ergo, it should help this group to have members of the same gender.
- *Registered students:* This service will be offered by the university's counseling services, and therefore all members must be registered students.
- *Lost relationship:* Because the purpose of the group is to help people cope effectively with a loss, it makes sense that members of the group should have sustained a lost relationship—and it should be a loss that they are finding some difficulty in managing.

With regard to the behavioral attributes listed previously:

- *Ability to verbalize feelings:* Some people can talk about strong feelings, others find it difficult to do so. In this group, it will be important to talk about a painful loss, so you hope to find some members who have found the strength to do so. These individuals could serve as models for others in the group who have more difficulty verbalizing their feelings.

- *Performance as a student:* Depression over a lost relationship is a normal part of life, but when it interferes with a person's ability to function as a student, something needs to be done about it. Some members may be able to manage their studies satisfactorily and could help others who are having problems with their role as students, so a mix of this attribute could be useful for the group.

- *Talk about their loss:* Potential members need to know and agree to the fact that this will be a discussion group, and that it is expected that they will participate in group discussion. We said that group members, however, should represent a mix of behavioral attributes. When we said "mix," we were referring to a range in relation to any particular behavioral attribute. This means you do not want a group in which everyone is so depressed that they cannot participate. Although all should be feeling unhappy about their loss, the group is likely to work better if members range along a continuum of "less depressed" to "more depressed" because the less depressed should be able to help those who are more depressed.

If everyone in a group is highly verbal, there may be insufficient "talk time" for everyone, whereas if everyone in the group has a tendency to clam up when in a group situation, you may have a very silent group! Again, a range of verbal participation styles seems likely to make for a group in which lively discussions can occur, and in which eventually the less verbal members will learn to tell their story, whereas the more talkative will learn to listen and learn as well as participate.

Sometimes one critical attribute is the most important of all and overrides the importance of other critical descriptive attributes. For example, this is an "oldie" but it makes the point. In the summer of 1961, one of us worked as a group facilitator in an institution for 110 women who were (to use the expression of that day) "pregnant out of wedlock." We were struck by the fact that in three groups with related but different purposes—orientation to the home, dealing with pregnancy and delivery, and planning for the postdelivery lives of themselves and their babies—extreme differences in age (12 through the mid-30s), race, and socioeconomic status did not interfere with communication between these women, all of whom were in the third trimester of their pregnancy. With the proliferation of support groups in today's world, a similar phenomenon has been observed in groups in which members all have the same major illness but differ widely with regard to descriptive attributes.

WHEN THE RULE DOES NOT APPLY

We also said that there are times when you ignore the maxim that members should be similar with regard to descriptive attributes and mixed as to behavioral attributes. One exception to the "similar-descriptive" rule is when the purpose of the group is to mix people with regard to their descriptive attributes for some particular reason.

Question: Please think of a situation in which you would want to deliberately mix people with significantly different descriptive attributes and describe it briefly.

Response: _____

_____

Here is one situation: To improve race relations among high school students, a group is composed in which members are deliberately selected because they differ with regard to race. The purpose of such a group is to provide opportunities for members of different races to meet, get to know and communicate with one another, and to learn from that experience. (Remember: When you compose a group with variations on one descriptive attribute, it is important to seek members who are similar with regard to other descriptive attributes such as age, grade in school, gender, and so on to the degree that you can.)

Here is another situation: Members of a homeowner's association who meet once every month to deal with neighborhood issues have noted that most members have children who are now adults. Given that there is an elementary school and a middle school within their neighborhood, they have decided that they need to change their composition to include younger members with children of school age.

These are cases in which we deliberately want to mix people with differing descriptive attributes. When you do this, however, you need to remember that members lack the initial affinity they would probably have if, for example, they were all of the same race, and you have to openly recognize—that is, tell the group—that differences may make it difficult, at first, for the group to "work." If you remind everyone of the reasons for mixing, however, and ask everyone to capitalize on the opportunities these differences provide, it should be possible for the group to develop.

With regard to behavioral attributes: At the beginning of this chapter, we referred to a number of interviews we held (as preparation for this second edition) with students and practitioners to learn about the kinds of experiences people were having with group composition in a variety of agencies. From these interviews, it became clear that practically no one was selecting members for treatment or support groups from a client pool by creating a balance of two or three critical behavioral attributes.[1] Sad! It sounded so good on paper. So "social scientific!" Once again, the real world intruded. We still think these concepts have merit, and it may even be possible to operationalize these ideas when composing a task group because task group chairpersons often have control over the group's membership. We just wanted you, the reader, to know that we recognize that reality is always present. Still, to put together a mix of people who do not belong together is irresponsible and potentially destructive, so each of you has to find your own middle ground if and when you attempt to implement the ideas we have presented in this chapter.

DESCRIPTIVE ATTRIBUTES—
A FURTHER NOTE

We said that unless the purpose of the group directs otherwise, you want to create a group whose members have similar descriptive attributes. We want to add a comment on what is meant by "similar" (or sharing a common descriptive attribute).

Question: You want to start a group for elementary school children who are experiencing difficulty in school, and you decide that a critical descriptive attribute would be the potential member's grade in school. Which of the following would you select as the best combination for the development of an effective group?

A. Only third-grade children
B. Only third- and fourth-grade children
C. Third- through fifth-grade children
D. Third- through sixth-grade children

Response: (select one)   A_____   B_____   C_____   D_____

Looking at these four choices, you might be inclined to feel that each choice would give you a group whose members are pretty similar with regard to the descriptive attribute "school grade." Actually, there is a world of difference between third and sixth graders: Ask them! To the sixth graders, most third graders are "babies," whereas to the third graders, sixth graders are generally viewed as "know-it-alls." They are not really similar populations. If there were enough third graders to select from for this group—that is, children having difficulty in school—we would stick with A. Often a child's grade is a function of his or her birthday, so that some third graders were not quite old enough, earlier, to be accepted into first grade, and they got a late start. Developmentally, however, third and fourth graders are pretty close, so alternative B might be acceptable. Again, however, the distance between third and fifth graders begins to be significant. Ask them!

This similarity business should never be taken for granted. To make the point, currently some Palestinians identify with the Palestinian Liberation Organization, some with the Islamic Jihad, and some with the Islamic Resistance Movement or Hamas. Trying to create a group from people who appear similar because you know them to be Palestinian could be a very dangerous business if the group's creator ignored the fundamental political differences currently existing between these groups.

Moral: The best way to determine similarity among people who appear to share a descriptive attribute is to ask them whether they themselves believe they are indeed similar. Failure to take this issue into account could result in some very uncomfortable (and unsuccessful) combinations of members.

BEHAVIORAL ATTRIBUTES—
A FURTHER NOTE

The contribution of Robert Freed Bales to the study of small groups is widely known. In 1950, he created a method for analyzing complex interactions in small groups, known as *interaction process analysis* (IPA) (Bales, 1950), which became widely accepted among social scientists. A later evolution of IPA was *systematic multiple level observation of groups* (SYMLOG) (Bales & Cohen, 1979), which has interesting implications for group composition.

In SYMLOG, Bales and Cohen (1979) postulated that all group members could be described in terms of three behavioral dimensions: (a) positive to negative patterns of interaction with others in the group; (b) the degree to which members share power, equally or unequally; and (c) the degree to which their behaviors range from task oriented to socioemotional. Bales and Cohen found that the most effective groups were those in which all members were essentially positive (friendly) in their interactions with others, shared power (rather than having a few dominant members), and were fairly task oriented—that is, were working actively to achieve individual or group goals or both.

Based on Bales and Cohen's (1979) observations, one could define these three dimensions as critical behavioral attributes and select members from a pool of potential members in relation to the behavioral attributes of friendliness, an ability to share power with others, and task orientation.

Persons interested in treatment groups will undoubtedly note that the pool they would encounter is not likely to contain many such individuals (who are friendly, task oriented, and prepared to share power) and they are probably right. Nevertheless, it is worth considering Bales and Cohen's work (assuming you have the luxury of taking behavioral attributes into account) when you compose a group, particularly in relation to task groups.

SUMMARY

When composing a group, you want to bring together people who have similar descriptive attributes but who differ with regard to behavioral attributes. Because people can be described in terms of dozens of attributes, you focus on just a few critical attributes that are selected because they are relevant to the purpose of the group. In selecting these attributes, you try to describe them as specifically as possible so they can be used with some precision when making decisions about group composition.

We recognize that there may be reasons for bending this rule. Putting people together with different descriptive attributes is often done to either create a more representative group or to fulfill the purpose of helping people get to know something about others who are different from themselves. We also suggested that assembling people with similar descriptive attributes requires one to check out similarity by asking people who you think to be similar whether they agree with your perception. Finally, we recognize that, although composing a group whose members represent a mix of people with a range of abilities with regard to a particular behavioral attribute may look good on paper, it simply does not happen very often in the real world. One more thing: All of the above may sound reasonable, but in many groups, particularly educational and task groups, you may have zero control over who shows. This will make it more difficult to turn a collection of people into an effective group, and you need to be prepared to come up with strategies that promote a feeling of "togetherness" as soon as possible if that is what you hope to achieve.

P.S.:
ATTRIBUTES OF THE FACILITATOR

Experience has shown that some facilitators prefer or are better than others, or both, working with particular populations—for example, children, senior citizens, terminally ill hospital patients, politically powerful board members, and so on. At the same time, potential members may initially experience greater comfort with (and thus be more willing to trust) a facilitator who is similar to them with regard to some particular descriptive attribute—for example, gender, race, age, and so on. Although the facilitator is not a member of the group, he or she is a central person in the group: Therefore, all of the considerations about group creation that have been presented so far have pertinence for matching the facilitator with the group. For example, a group of African American men who are assigned a European American female facilitator starts with some compositional issues that may be very difficult to manage, regardless of that person's skills as a group facilitator.[2]

Of particular interest are those groups in which members are deliberately mixed in terms of descriptive attributes, which we discussed previously. Brown and Mistry (1994) make the point that in such groups, it is advisable to use a cofacilitator arrangement in which the facilitators are chosen because they are each characterized by the same descriptive attributes as the members. Therefore, in a group whose purpose is to improve relationships between Christians and Jews, for example, one facilitator should be Christian and the other Jewish. Furthermore, the facilitators should be coequal rather than having one facilitator who is clearly dominant. The realities of practice may make such an arrangement appear impractical, but we believe that this kind of coleadership is desirable; without it, it is less likely that this collection of people will become an effective group.

Task groups that are deliberately mixed with regard to descriptive attributes to be representative of diverse populations place a particularly difficult burden on a facilitator. If the facilitator is identified as belonging to one of these populations, he or she must struggle with an image that he or she might favor that population. On the other hand, the facilitator may be dissimilar to all of the populations represented. In such a situation, the facilitator needs to learn about each of the populations and always recognize the potential for divisiveness these differences can create.

NOTES

1. Several indicated, however, that poor group composition was the major problem they experienced in working with their groups.

2. On the other hand, if these men are competitive over issues of power, not having a male facilitator to compete with might make such an arrangement work, providing the white female facilitator is comfortable with and skilled in performing her position as group facilitator with a group of black men. For an interesting discussion of this issue, see Davis (1995).

A MIDSTREAM SUPPLICATION

Reader: As you read, empha-*size* what is i-*tal*-icized.

The *im*-pact of a *text* on pro-
Fes-sional per-*for*-mance, is
Of-ten not *much*—that's
Sad but *true*. What
Us-ually inter-*feres* (and we've
Seen it through the *years*) are the
Mul-titude of *tasks* that your
Job makes you *do*.

Not 'nough *time* to do it *right,* like cre-
Ate a client *pool,* from
Which you can se-*lect* the
Ver-y best *mix*. So you
take who is a-*vail*-able, to
Whom the group is *sal*-able, and
Put them all to-*geth*-er, hoping
You've achieved a *"fix."*

Nonethe-*less* we will con-*tin*-ue to pre-
Sent our i-*deas,* de-
Scrib-ing group cre-*a*-tion in a
Way we hope is *fun*. We'll ex-
Pand upon our *teach*-ing (with a
Lit-tle bit of *preach*-ing) and we
Hope you'll keep on *read*-ing til the
Book is *done*.

6

GROUP MODIFICATION

In group creation, you select members for a group that does not yet exist. In group modification, the composition of an existing group is changed because

1. New members "arrive" as a natural process of the setting in which the group exists, or because you or the group, or both, decide to add new members.
2. Members "graduate" or depart, or you deliberately remove some current members.

Question: Briefly describe a specific circumstance you can think of, for each kind of group, in which new members join an existing group. Then briefly describe a specific circumstance for each kind of group in which current members leave an existing group.

Response: New members join an existing group when:

Treatment: _____

_____

Support: _____

_____

Educational: _____

_____

Task: _____

_____

Current members leave an existing group when:

Treatment: _____

_____

Support: _____

_____

Educational: _____

_____

Task: _____

_____

We consider any of the following answers to be appropriate. New members would join an existing group when

- The facilitator or the facilitator and the group together decide that the group needs one or more new members whose attributes could make the group more effective. Indeed, some would argue that addition of new members should only be done with the participation of the group's members and never by the facilitator alone.
- In the setting in which the group exists, new members are regularly added to the group, and current members rotate out of the group. For example, in a residential setting, such as a hospital, a patient's stay is limited to 28 days, and new members are added as they come into residence, or, on a committee, membership is time limited by the rules of the committee, and new members are added to take their place.
- A new member is added when a person who has been a member achieves his or her individual goal(s) and graduates or a member fails to achieve his or her individual goals to such a significant degree that it is decided by the facilitator that he or she should leave the group. (Either situation creates room for new members.)
- The facilitator believes that the group is too small to be effective (with regard to achieving its purpose or the group's goals or both) and in a planning session with the group it is decided to enlarge the group.

- In a support group, an individual who has heard about the group shows up unannounced, to participate in a meeting, to decide whether or not he or she wants to join as a regularly attending member. Support groups are unique in that the composition of group membership is often not something that the group or the facilitator can control, providing the new member "fits" a critical descriptive attribute required for membership in a particular group—that is, the new member is an ex-psychiatric hospital patient in a support group for ex-psychiatric hospital patients.

Perhaps you have thought of other reasons for changing membership by introducing new members.

Members would leave an existing group when

- Membership is time limited, and their time is up.
- A member decides to withdraw from the group because he or she believes it is not meeting his or her needs or because the group is not achieving one or more group goals of importance to that member.
- External circumstances force a member to leave—for example, the member moves away.

Again, you may have thought of other situations in which members leave an existing group.

Note that arrival and departure of members of an existing group is not always controlled by the group's facilitator(s). Nonetheless, we present the following principle that pertains to group modification:

The more the facilitator or the facilitator and the group can control who enters the group, the greater the possibility that they can use arrivals and departures to make the group more effective.[1]

In other words, the more a facilitator or the facilitator and the group allow or are forced to allow circumstances beyond their control to determine who enters or leaves a group, the more difficulty the facilitator will have in helping the group to become effective.

In the discussion that follows, we suggest two factors to be considered when group modifications occurs. Actually, these factors also pertain to planning for group creation. They include the following:

1. Selecting potential members on the basis of previously demonstrated ability to perform either task or group socioemotional roles in a group (this is discussed in detail below).
2. Selecting potential members who can serve as good role models for others to emulate (again, this is discussed in detail below).

TASK AND
SOCIOEMOTIONAL ROLES

Let's discuss task and socioemotional (also referred to as "group main-tenance") roles first. Research on small groups has indicated that a group needs two special functions to be performed if a group is to survive and develop—that is, both must be going on throughout the life of the group (Forsyth, 1990). The task function has to do with working toward the achievement of the group's purposes and the specific goals its members develop for it and includes behaviors such as making suggestions, sharing experiences relevant to prior attempts at problem solving, and so on. This sort of work is referred to as *task activity. Socioemotional activity* involves keeping the group together and involves behaviors such as effect-ing compromises, soothing hurt feelings, rewarding constructive partici-pation, and so on.

For example, a person who is well organized when attempting to solve problems might perform a task activity such as suggesting a way of organizing problem solving for a group. If the group is time limited in nature, this behavioral attribute might be critical for the group to be successful with regard to achieving its goals. On the other hand, an individual who is known as a "wheeler-dealer" in the community might perform some essential task activities for a group whose goal is to bring about community change.

Socioemotional abilities that a group might need are often less related to the group's purposes or goals than to the characteristic behavioral patterns of its members. For example, in a group with a few verbally assertive members, adding one or more calm, yet dedicated members may help the group navigate troubled waters by, for example, softening harsh phrases some members might use. On the other hand, if a group includes several members who are reluctant to participate, a member who can crack a joke could ease the group atmosphere with a resultant increase in widespread participation. Socioemotional behaviors, then, have less to do with solving problems than with keeping members together, in good harmony, while they interact around solving the group's problems.

Question: Which of the following behaviors would you categorize as task behaviors (T), and which would you categorize as socioemotional behav-iors (S)?

Response: (circle the appropriate designation)

  1. Frequently praises other people's comments. T or S

2. Has a fund of funny stories that others find relaxing. T or S
3. Is good at summarizing what others have been saying. T or S
4. Is good at working out compromises between people who disagree. T or S
5. Is able to come up with novel ways for solving a problem. T or S
6. Is good at locating information that the group needs. T or S

Check your answers: 3, 5, and 6 are task behaviors because they help the group to move toward that achievement of individual or group goals, or both, whereas 1, 2, and 4 are socioemotional behaviors because they help members work together better while they are struggling to accomplish these individual or group goals or both.

MODELING

Modeling refers to a process in which an individual learns new behaviors by imitating the behaviors of another person and then adapting the observed demonstration to his or her own style.

Example. Albert might be invited to join because it has been observed that he is able to control his temper in tense situations. This may be important because Bill, who already is a member, cannot control his temper and needs to see how it is done effectively by a peer.

Example. Jane might be invited to join a group for psychiatric hospital patients who are approaching discharge because she has considerable work experience, has been out of the hospital for 6 months, is doing well in her job, and is interested in participating to help these patients (some of whom she knows) succeed once they are back in the community. In looking for members of a treatment group, do not limit yourself to individuals who are still clients of your agency. People who have graduated from the agency are an excellent source of role modeling. In addition, graduates often feel good about themselves when they are able to help clients who are still in a treatment program.

Example. In a representative task group, constituency groups might be asked if they could locate an individual with considerable experience in managing the finances of this particular kind of group.

Example. In an in-service training group, a facilitator might look for a staff member with experience in working with disabled persons because the group has expressed an interest in learning how to work with this population.

SUMMARY

When modifying an existing group, you should try to determine whether your group could use new members with good task or socioemotional skills, or who could serve as good role models of particular kinds of behavior. Because these are both behavioral attributes, you may have to rely on self-reports of potential members or reports from reliable sources who are familiar with the behavioral patterns of these potential members.

Based on our earlier discussions, you would most likely want to add new members whose descriptive attributes are similar to those of current group members, unless the purpose of the group is to mix people according to their descriptive attributes.

P.S.

The decision to remove a treatment group member because he or she has made no progress toward personal goal achievement, or to replace a task group member because his or her presence is interfering with the group's goal achievement, is a very serious move and should be thought through carefully. The following example refers to a group that saw itself as a task group, which they were, but that was also seen (secretly) by the facilitator as having an important treatment component.

Example. A cross-age tutoring program was created in an elementary school in which sixth graders who were having difficulty with schoolwork were recruited to serve as tutors for first graders who were having difficulty with schoolwork. Unfortunately, their facilitator only told them they had been selected to serve as tutors because it was thought they could be of help to the first graders. The facilitator carefully avoided telling them that the group had a dual purpose—to help the first graders and to help the sixth graders by giving them a positive role (for the first time) to play in school. The tutors met weekly with the facilitator to discuss their tutoring. It soon became clear that one tutor, Carl, was doing a very poor job with his tutee. The other tutors voted to expel Carl from the tutoring group and find a replacement. The facilitator then had to explain the dual purpose of the group and ask the group to help Carl rather than expel him. The facilitator apologized for her deception and explained that she was afraid that none of the tutors would have agreed to join the group if they had known of the group's dual purpose. Fortunately, the members were sufficiently committed to their tutees to stay on, but a chastened facilitator learned an old lesson: Honesty is the best policy.

This is but one example of why one should be cautious about expelling a group member "for the good of the group."

Removing an individual from a task group because, for example, that individual has continually sidetracked the group when action needed to be taken, is very difficult, especially if that member is a representative of a particular constituency. In fact, such a removal may be impossible. In this type of case, the facilitator should consider adopting the strategy of strengthening the rest of the group's ability to stay on topic, thus neutralizing the sidetracking member's impact on the group.

Question: Can you think of instances in which it would be appropriate to remove a member from a group?

1. _____

_____

2. _____

_____

3. _____

_____

The following are some possible scenarios in which the removal of a member may be the best step to take:

- The facilitator learns that the member's attributes were not what they appeared to be when the member was first recruited, making the group inappropriate for this individual—for example, a young woman joined a short-term abortion counseling group for pregnant women and reported that she was pregnant. In time, it was learned that she was not pregnant, but had joined the group to learn about the process of abortion. Because the agency had groups that would explain abortions and other issues concerning pregnancy to women who were not pregnant, it was decided to move her to one of those groups.

- In a task group, an individual joined the group claiming to be a representative of a particular population. In time, it was discovered that the individual did not actually represent that population, so that that population remained underrepresented. The group decided to remove the individual who was not truly representative of that population and replace the individual with someone who was.

- It was discovered that (unknown to the facilitator) an already formed subgroup had been recruited to the group, and that within the group, the subgroup functioned in such a way as to obstruct the group's progress. To protect the group's development, some of the subgroup members were moved to another group.

Obviously, the issues pertaining to the decision to deliberately remove a member from a group are complex and should be thought through with care.

SUMMARY

Group modification is the term we use for midstream changes in a group's composition. Sometimes it occurs when the facilitator and the group together decide to add a member who could provide a new and needed resource; at other times, the facilitator and the group have to deal with issues associated with one or more member's departure from the group. Experience suggests that the more group modification occurs within the control of the facilitator and the group, the more likely an effective group will develop or be maintained.

NOTE

1. One could argue that the facilitator cannot—indeed should not—control which person a constituency of a task group selects for group membership. In response, we say that the facilitator can, quite appropriately, indicate the kind of person this group needs without intruding on that constituency's ultimate control of its own process for selecting its representative.

7

TIME, SIZE, AND SPACE

In planning for a group, some important details need to be addressed.

Time
How often should the group meet?
How long should each meeting run?
Should the group be time limited—for example, one meeting, eight meet-
ings, and so on—or ongoing—that is, members change over time, but
the group goes on and on?
Size
How large should the group be? (minimum size—two; maximum—?)
Should the size vary from time to time, depending on what the group is
doing?
Space
Where should the group meet?

This chapter will address these questions.

TIME

There is no optimum time plan that fits every group, but there are some
guidelines that can be used when trying to select time arrangements
pertaining to any one group.

Question: What factors do you think would need to be considered when
selecting a time plan for any group? (Hint: One obvious factor is purpose.

Once you have determined a group's purpose you can at least make a stab at trying to determine how long it should take a group to accomplish its purpose.) What else? A is our response to this question. B, C, and D should be yours.

A. Purpose—Once you know what the group's purpose is, you can estimate how long it should take a group to accomplish that purpose.

B. _____

_____

C. _____

_____

D. _____

_____

The following are some of the factors we think you should consider:

- The sponsoring organization's experience with this kind of group (assuming there is some such experience) and what it tells about optimum time factors—the Leukemia Foundation conducted a pilot telephone support group for six women who had leukemia. It ran for 6 successive weeks, meeting by conference phone, for 1-hour-long meetings. After the group terminated, an evaluation of the program discovered that members had found the group useful ("useful" in the sense that they had never before had anyone to talk to who shared the same illness they had—now they had begun the process of talking about and getting new ideas from one another about how to manage their illness more effectively) and had found 1-hour-long meetings appropriate ("appropriate" in the sense that the members reported feeling that they had ample time to both talk about themselves and hear from all of the other members), but thought the number of meetings was too few ("too few" in the sense that each felt that she had made insufficient progress toward achieving her goals of improved management of her illness, and that more meetings would have brought her closer to goal achievement). Although it was obviously a "guesstimate," both members and facilitators thought that 10 or 12 meetings would have been more productive. Incidentally, if your organization has had no experience with a particular kind of group, some other organization in the community that had such an experience could be consulted.

- The nature of the task the group is undertaking could have an important relationship to time factors. If this is a one-shot orientation group, what needs to be determined is the amount of information to be delivered, understood and acquired, and how long that will take. A support group is almost always open ended with regard to time with no finite time limits. Although regular individual participation is encouraged, members come or do not come to meetings as they will, but the group is always available. On the other hand, a committee often has particular deadlines to meet, and these deadlines contribute to decisions about when, how often, and for how long the group should meet. With today's emphasis on short-term treatment groups (one to three meetings), the goals that members select have to be informed by the limited time there is to achieve them.

- Member availability can affect a group's time plans. For example, in a support group for visually impaired elderly, the fact that they all needed transportation to the meeting and often could not afford taxis to and from the meeting (and therefore had to rely on scarce volunteer drivers) dictated a once-a-month meeting plan.

- Organizational time limits affect time factors for many groups. For example, a 28-day inpatient facility for substance abusers has much to accomplish in a comparatively short time period, but with potential members available 24 hours a day, meetings are scheduled for 2 or 3 hours at a time, daily, for at least 5 days a week.

- Planning for a group's time may be a function of tradition—that is, "We've always done it this way." This is sometimes a poor reason for making decisions about time and may need to be challenged (or at least rethought), but it is often an important determinant.

- Once the group has begun to meet, members should have the right to modify the existing time arrangement to fit their needs. For example, staff who are participating in a training group might, once the group is assembled, decide on a different time pattern for the group that better fits their work schedules than the original time plan for the group. Another example is that members of a treatment group might decide that meeting once a week is insufficient, in terms of the immediate demands all are facing, and decide to meet three times a week.

Perhaps you have thought of other factors that would affect time arrangements for the group you are creating; in planning for group creation, however, decisions about time should be made that are known and acceptable to all who are involved and, in addition, feasible to administer.

SIZE

As we indicated earlier, just about every definition of the word group uses the phrase, "two or more (members) . . ." but fails to specify what number is meant by the "or more" phrase. This can probably be traced to the fact that groups come in all sorts of sizes depending on a number of factors. As a creator of a group, you will need to give careful thought to the issue of group size, and having done so, operate on the basis of your best guess about the size you hope will work best for you.

One factor you will want to consider is the way in which the size of a group creates a particular number of relationships for each member to manage. For example, in a group of two (or, as it is technically known, a *dyad*) there is only one relationship for each member to manage—that is, A interacts with B, and B interacts with A. In a three-member group (a *triad*), however, A and B interact, A and C interact, and B and C interact. In other words, adding only one member increases the number of relationships each person has to manage by two. In a group of four, there are six relationships to be managed, and so on.

Question: How many relationships does each participant[1] have to manage in a group of six members and one facilitator?

Response: (select one)　　A. 14　　　　B. 21　　　　C. 42

The correct answer is B or 21, which is a lot of relationships to manage!

There is a simple way to calculate this number. Take the number of participants (in this case, 6 members and 1 facilitator make for a total of 7 participants), multiply it by the number of participants minus 1 (in this case, 6, which means $7 \times 6 = 42$), and divide by 2 (in this case, $42 \div 2 = 21$) and you have the total number of potential relationships in a group of that size. Try this formula ($N \times N - 1 \div 2$) and you can easily arrive at the number of potential relationships in any group. For a group of 10 members and 1 facilitator? We are sure you have got it and know this answer is 55. Correct! Again, that is a lot of relationships for each participant (including the facilitator, by the way) to manage.

(For the arithmetically sophisticated, one could say that as a group's size increases arithmetically, the number of potential relationships increases geometrically. A bit of unimportant trivia with which to impress your friends.)

It is important to add that not every participant relates with equal intensity to every other participant. In fact, studies of small groups that focus on affectional patterns in groups often find members liking some of the other members, being indifferent to some, and disliking some.[2] Therefore, our formula only indicates the number of potential relationships in a group as determined by its size. Remember, however, that facilitators of a group are expected to develop positive working relationships with every group member. In addition, the fewer the number of positive relationships within a group, the lower the group's cohesiveness (defined as the sum total of all participants' attraction to the group) (Forsyth, 1990, pp. 10-11). As a group's cohesiveness increases, several changes are seen: Members like, trust, and respect one another more, have more of a "we-feeling," are more likely to be influenced by one another, are more likely to be satisfied with the group, are more likely to participate more fully and communicate more frequently, are more likely to experience heightened self-esteem and lowered anxiety, are less likely to miss meetings, and are more likely to remain a member over time (Forsyth, 1990). In short, the cohesive group is an effective group, which is what every facilitator hopes to achieve.

Question: Which of the following statements pertaining to group size would you consider to be valid? (Circle the identifying letter for statements you consider to be valid.)

A. As a group's size increases, the group becomes more efficient.

B. As a group's size increases, relationships among members become more complex.

C. As a group's size increases, the group needs more structure to perform effectively.

D. As a group's size increases, members who are shy about participation are better able to remain relatively nonparticipative in the group.

E. As a group's size increases, more subgroups are likely to develop within it.

F. As a group's size increases, the group's ability to undertake complex tasks will automatically improve.

G. As a group's size increases, each member will have more relationships with which to cope.

Let's discuss these points one by one, but the correct answers are (i.e., the valid statements are) B, C, D, E, and G.

A. No. A group's efficiency is more likely to be a function of the way in which it is organized than of its size. It is often the case that groups actually become less efficient as they increase in size because the group is not sufficiently well organized to cope with the increase in the number of relationships each participant must manage.

B. Yes. The complexity that accompanies an increase in size is directly associated with the number of relationships each participant must manage in whatever the group does.

C. Yes. "Structure" means the pattern of relationships in a group. It has been found that the larger the group, the more relationships need to be patterned in predictable ways if the group is to be effective (Forsyth, 1990, p. 220). This usually means that members will have to agree on more rules for the group as group size increases.

D. Yes. Research has shown that the more members participate in a group, the more likely they are to be affected by what goes on in the group (Forsyth, 1990, pp. 9, 129-139). It is clear that individual change is an important outcome a facilitator hopes to achieve when working with a treatment, support, or educational group. If a member does not participate, however, he or she is less likely to be changed by the group experience. In our view, this means that individual change may not occur for nonparticipating members if a group gets too large. Unfortunately, some individuals in larger groups often do not participate. In effect, they hide in the crowd and thus do not benefit from the group experience. One could almost postulate a rule: The larger the group, the more nonparticipating members there will be (unless, of course, the facilitator acts to overcome this tendency). Low or nonparticipating members sometimes disagree with this view, saying that they were listening very carefully, even though they did not say much. Until they participate, however, there is no way to determine how the group has affected them. Accordingly, we prefer a small group (four to nine) when a major purpose of the group is to bring about individual change.[3]

E. Yes. The fact that subgroups are more likely to develop in large groups than in small groups is not necessarily a problem, but it is a fact. Subgroups can be beneficial provided they give each member a sense of belonging to a component of the larger group. They can become a problem if some members remain isolates. If that happens, you may want to facilitate interaction that brings isolates into membership in a subgroup.

F. No. The key word here is "automatically." Often, groups, particularly task groups, need to be larger to work on the resolution of a complex problem. Larger groups provide a wider diversity of perspectives and experiences that can be useful in solving complex problems. If the group has not developed a well-operating structure, however, the larger it gets, the clumsier it gets.

G. Yes. This statement simply reiterates the point we made earlier—the larger the group, the more relationships each member will confront. In a treatment or a support group, if a group gets too large, there may be too many relationships for each member to manage, and the group may lose effectiveness. Educational and task groups, on the other hand, may do well with increased size for reasons mentioned previously. What do we mean by "large" and "small?" A small group would be 4 to 9, whereas a large group could be anywhere from 10 to 30.[4] Above 30, the group begins to become a crowd, and we are not writing about crowds.

Having made this point, we need to report a group approach in which 30 members is considered the largest feasible size, but one (i.e., 30) that is workable. Bell (1995) describes a one-session, 2- or 3-hour group approach, called *traumatic event debriefing* (TED), for from 3 to 30 individuals who have shared one traumatic event—for example, a natural catastrophe (such as an earthquake), an accidental catastrophe (such as a plane crash), or a "human-induced" catastrophe (such as the murder of a staff member while at work). Staff for these sessions (known as "debriefers") should number between two and four, although five or more may be appropriate for larger groups.

Moral: Rules about group size always have to take into account the reality of the group's purpose for existence.

MEETING SITE

Question: Groups come in so many sizes and shapes, meet for such a wide variety of purposes, and meet in such diverse settings that it is difficult to establish guidelines for a meeting site. Therefore, let's begin with the following question: What is the worst meeting site you have ever encountered?

Nature/purpose of group? _____

Nature of meeting site? _____

What made it so bad? _____

_____

The following are some of the sites we have seen that just did not work and, in fact, made it almost impossible to have an effective group:

- In a special education class of eight boys and six girls, ages 13 to 15, the girls were invited to participate in a group to discuss problems of concern to young women. The group met in the back of the classroom, behind a 6-foot partition that did nothing to prevent the boys from overhearing every word spoken. Due to this lack of privacy, none of the girls wanted to speak up, and the group was a dismal failure.

- A group for men with AIDS was scheduled to meet in a local community center, but the members (all of whom were gay) found this kind of public exposure uncomfortable, and most chose to not attend.
- Members of a group for the elderly visually impaired met around several thin tables in a row, arranged as one long "Thanksgiving-like" table. This arrangement made it difficult for them to hear one another, and the meeting went nowhere.

We could go on, listing rooms that were too small, too noisy, even rooms that were "double-booked" so that another group was in the room when your group arrived.

The fact is that an inappropriate meeting site can have an extremely negative effect on any group.

Perhaps the examples we have selected have suggested some guidelines for a meeting site that could fit any group. Let's see.

Question: What are at least three criteria for selection of a meeting site?

1. _____

   _____

2. _____

   _____

3. _____

   _____

The following are some guidelines for selecting a group's meeting site that we think are important. See how they compare with yours.

1. *Privacy:* It is certainly true of treatment and support groups that they stress confidentiality—"What's said here stays here." In a different vein, task groups often deal in problem solving with regard to politically sensitive issues and may prefer that their work on solving these problems remains private until some kind of consensus has been achieved. Educational groups want privacy to avoid distractions.

2. *Audibility:* It is important that members can hear one another, which means a meeting site in which external sources of noise do not interfere with the group's interactions.

3. *Comfort:* Members are often together for 1 or 2 hours, and it helps one and all if everyone is physically comfortable during that time.

4. *Distractions:* In some groups, members are easily distracted if they are surrounded by paraphernalia such as balls to throw and ropes to swing on, such as you find in a gymnasium, and so on. When the meeting is set to include active physical interaction—for example, game playing—that is fine, but at other times it just gets in the way.

5. *Size:* A small group, meeting in a corner of a large auditorium, may feel less comfortable than that same small group meeting in a room that is just large enough for it. One of us worked (in the early 1960s) with a group of adolescent boys in a street gang and found that some of his best meetings took place in his station wagon at night, which could only accommodate 8 boys at most. (When the total gang met, up to 25 boys were present.) Incidentally, he found that the boys reported feeling safe in his car even when, or especially when, he drove through "enemy territory" and seemed better able to talk there because (a) in relation to the total gang, this was a small group in which they could have a chance to be heard, and (b) the environment of the station wagon created a situation in which they were not involved in eye-to-eye interaction with the facilitator (who was busy driving the vehicle) and with each other, which seemed to make it easier for them to talk about personal matters. In this example, factors of group size combined with a unique site (for a group meeting) to facilitate communication.

6. *Relevance:* In describing TED (see above), Bell (1995) writes,

> TEDs do not take place in a therapist's office. Instead they are conducted at a facility close to where the victims live or work. This concept of providing service in the client's own environment is familiar to social workers experienced in outreach and home visits. (p. 41)

SUMMARY

When planning for a group's creation, the group's facilitator has to consider factors of time, size, and space. Unfortunately, there are no hard and fast rules (such as the belief that the ideal size for a task group is X. Sorry! There is no such rule, except that you probably want an odd number of members, so there will never be a 50/50 vote!).[5] Again, decisions on matters of time, size, and space are best made by referring to the group's purpose.

NOTES

1. In any group, participants include the members plus the facilitator(s). Therefore, a treatment group with 8 members and 2 facilitators would involve 10 participants.

2. Affectional patterns in groups have been studied using sociometric methods of analysis. See Forsyth (1990, pp. 33-35).

3. It has been our personal observation that even adding one more person (for a total of 10) leads to a significant drop in a treatment group's effectiveness. On the other hand, a group of 4 runs the risk of becoming almost no group at all if a couple of members are absent.

4. We have heard of support groups of 12 members, but that gets to be pretty big, with the result that some individual members can get "lost." Therefore, we will stick with 9 as a top size for treatment and support groups. Note that there are plenty of people who would disagree.

5. Even here there is room for discussion. For example, in a task group of nine—which is an odd number—a vote of 5 against 4 does provide a majority, but it is so close that the group might do better to go back and rework the issue until something approaching consensus exists. In a recent vote for board chair of the National Association for the Advancement of Colored People (NAACP), the new chair was elected by a vote of 30 to 29 (*Detroit Free Press,* February 20, 1995). This vote meant that the old leadership lost, but such a close vote did not augur well for the board's future problem-solving body.

8

COMPOSING A GROUP

Our final two chapters will focus on one kind of group. This specificity will provide the reader with concrete examples of the composition of a group from a pool, and the planning needed for a first meeting, to help a collection of strangers become a developing group.[1]

For our example, we are using a treatment group that was composed by a school social worker. The school setting is one environment in which groups are used extensively. Counselors, teachers, student assistance workers, school social workers, and other professionals, as well as some non-professionals (volunteers), lead groups with titles such as Children of Divorce, Survivors of Attempted Suicide, Adolescent Issues Group, Positive Peer Culture or Guided Group Interaction Groups, Insight Groups, Children of Alcoholics, and Social Competency Groups.

The school setting offers helpers a significant amount of choice regarding the process of selecting group members. Recruitment of members can be done by advertising, through referral agents, or by word of mouth from student to student.

IDENTIFYING A PURPOSE
FOR THE GROUP

In the example we have chosen, a social worker (we will call her Ruth Morgan) was assigned to a high school with about 1,200 students. She circulated a questionnaire to a sample of the student body to get a sense of the issues that were of concern to students. Responses indicated high levels of suicidal thoughts and concern about substance abuse. Ruth decided to offer services that might prevent future increases of these problems in the school by focusing on normal developmental needs of adolescents. She reasoned that if the stresses involved at this point of the normal life cycle could be reduced, students would be less likely to turn to drugs or consider suicide. She decided to focus on positive desired outcomes by offering groups to students who wanted to learn how to improve their relationships with peers or adults.

Question: After developing this rationale, what do you think should be Ruth's next step in creating groups?

A.____ Recruiting coworkers.
B.____ Posting an announcement to recruit members.
C.____ Seeking administrative approval for this type of group.
D.____ Finding a room for meetings.

Answer: You will remember our earlier discussion about an environment of acceptance, so we think the correct answer is C. As a matter of fact, the use of treatment groups was a tradition in this school, so Ruth had no trouble getting approval for the group from school administrators. Accordingly, she posted the sign depicted in Box 8.1 on school bulletin boards. Twenty-two students volunteered to be in a group, necessitating the formation of more than one group.

Box 8.1. Notice

A group is being formed for students who would like to find out how to improve their relationships with peers or adults. If you would like to join such a group, please sign up by writing "Relationship Group," your name and telephone number on a piece of paper, and slipping it under Ruth Morgan's door, Room 116. Ms. Morgan is one of our school's social workers. She will call you to confirm receiving your request and to answer any questions you may have about the group.

Question: How many groups would you compose from 22 students?

A. ___ Six
B. ___ Five
C. ___ Four
D. ___ Three
E. ___ Two

Answer: We select C or D as the correct answer. A group of 11 (response E) would be too large, and six groups (response A) would lead to some groups of 3, which are too small. In addition, five groups (response B) would have 4 members in all but two groups, which would not provide for enough members if someone was absent for one meeting.

To decide whether to compose three or four groups, Ruth reviewed her purpose for the group in relation to three critical descriptive attributes: gender, race, and grade in school. There were 12 female and 10 male volunteers. Ruth could make four groups, with two for males and two for females.

Question: Would this meet her goal of improving relationships with peers through working in a group?   Yes _____   No _____

Answer: We do not think so. Building relationships across gender is part of the normal life cycle stresses among high school students, and a group would be an excellent place for learning how to improve cross-gender relationships. Therefore, we want groups that mix genders. To mix genders for each group, Ruth decided to compose three groups that would stress race and grade in school as common descriptive attributes.

Question: Of these two attributes, which would be most important in relation to meeting the groups' major purpose of improving relationships with peers?

A. ___ Race
B. ___ Grade in school

Ruth wanted members in the same grade to develop more and better relationships with each other. She was not as concerned about improving relationships between 10th and 11th graders. She wanted the students to have more close friends among the peers with whom they spent most of the day and hoped that the in-group relationships could more easily transfer out of the group.

She also wanted to be sure there were both European American and African American students in each group to break down some of the barriers between the races in the school.[2]

Question: Does the mixing of the races fit our earlier recommendation of composing groups with common descriptive attributes?

A. ____ Yes
B. ____ No

Answer: No, it does not. Making the decision to have mixed-race groups, however, does fit our continuing emphasis on group purpose as the final measure for decisions about composing groups.

Using the common attribute of grade in school, Ruth was able to tentatively form three groups, as shown below.

Group 1—Sophomores
    Three female European American students
    Two female African American students
    One male European American student
    Two male African American students
Group 2—Juniors
    Two female African American students
    Two female European American students
    One male African American student
    Three male European American students
Group 3—Seniors
    Three female European American students
    Two male African American students
    One male European American student

Question: Once three tentative groups had been composed, Ruth wanted each member of a group to have all three descriptive attributes in common with at least one other group member. As you look at Group 1 for sophomores, where has this principle not been achieved? (Write your answer below.)

Answer: One male European American student.

Question: What would be a good way to deal with this lack of a member who is matched with someone else having common descriptive attributes?

A. ____ Drop him from the group.

B. ____ Add another male European American student from Ruth's caseload.

C. ____ Invite this member to bring a friend of the same gender and race.

Answer: All three answers would create the balance necessary for common descriptive attributes among at least two members. Dropping him from the group, however, would deprive the group of any representation of European American males. Also, it would entail finding another way to provide service to this volunteer because a worker is obligated to provide resources of some kind to every student who voluntarily seeks help.

Looking at Groups 2 and 3, Ruth realized that she would have to either recruit one more member to each group or drop the member who lacked all three descriptive attributes in common with at least one other member.

Question: She knew her final decision could wait until after which of the following had been carried out?

A. ____ Finding rooms for the three groups.

B. ____ The first group meeting.

C ____ Screening interviews with each potential member.

D. ____ Obtaining parental permission for students to participate in the group.

E. ____ Finding facilitators for the groups.

Answer: Both C and D are correct. Conducting the screening interview allows the student to make a verbal commitment to participate in the group and allows the facilitator an opportunity to determine if the student seems to be able to benefit from a group. The final step in joining a group is obtaining parental permission. Until Ruth had obtained commitments from the students, she did not know how many rooms would be needed, how many group facilitators would be needed, and if there would even be a first meeting.

As discussed earlier, the best indicator of whether someone can benefit from a group is his or her past experience in small groups. If there has been one or more negative experiences, the facilitator needs to explore how the potential participant expects this experience to be different.

When potential members have had very little (or no) previous treatment group experience, the best measure of a potential successful experience is based on their beliefs about the likely helpfulness of this new small group experience. One way to determine an individual's beliefs is to structure a screening interview using a brief questionnaire just prior to the interview. Ruth developed the one shown in Box 8.2.

Box 8.2.

This brief questionnaire is intended to determine your commitment to change and your willingness to learn how to help others to change. Please place a check at the appropriate point on each scale below:

1. How high is your commitment to changing at least one relationship that concerns you?

High   Somewhat   Low

2. How high is your confidence that these group meetings will help you in improving your relationships with peers and/or adults?

High   Somewhat   Low

3. How high is your confidence that learning how to help others improve their relationships with peers and/or adults will help you learn to do the same thing?

High   Somewhat   Low

After each student had filled out the questionnaire, Ruth conducted the screening interview. She first probed for more information regarding each of the three dimensions listed on her questionnaire.

Question: Which questions listed below would fit one or more of the dimensions?

A. ___ "In this group we will be working on helping each other change or grow. Is this what you want to have happen for yourself?"

B. ___ "Our group will really delve into each other's past. Is that okay with you?"

C. ___ "This group will share some ways each member has used to build relationships with peers or adults. Will that be helpful to you? In what way?"

D. ___ "Do you think helping others will be helpful to you? Please explain your answer."

Answer: A, C, and D. These three questions emphasize the specific purposes Ruth had for the group. These are

1. Focus on the present, and work on changing it.
2. Use the group to help individuals achieve change.
3. Help one another to improve self-esteem and ability to change.

Answer B, seeking information on the past, will not be the major focus of the group. Past experiences will certainly be brought up by group members, but only as they seem connected to situations they are experiencing now.

In addition to sharing the major purposes of the group with each potential member, Ruth described the basic structure of the meetings. She wanted each student to have clear expectations regarding what would happen during the meetings.

Question: Which of the following statements would provide members with clear expectations for each meeting?

A. ___ "We'll talk about each other's problems with relationships and give each other advice."

B. ___ "At every meeting we'll try to help at least one person with a relationship problem."

C. ___ "Meetings will involve planning our own time together, working on relationships, and reviewing the progress of our group."

Answer: B and C are clear explanations of what will happen at a meeting. A is too problem focused, and giving advice—that is, telling someone what they should do—is something you want to avoid in a treatment group.

After sharing these purposes and expectations, Ruth asked each volunteer to decide whether they wanted to participate in a group. Eventually, she accepted all 22 volunteers because they were all firmly committed to working on relationships through participation in a group, and each had obtained permission from his or her parents to be in one of these groups.

Ruth decided to recruit volunteers from her caseload to achieve a balance in each group with regard to gender and race.

Question: Which of the following reasons would justify such a decision?

A. ___ Asking one student to bring a friend of the same race and gender would make that pair of members unique from all other members.

B. ___ Bringing a friend could set up an alliance between the pair that would tend to exclude other group members.

C. ___ Selecting students from her caseload would allow her to offer group services to those who lacked peer relationship skills.

D. ___ Selecting a member would help Ruth keep control of group meetings.

Answer: A and B are both sound reasons to avoid asking a member to bring a friend. C is an excellent reason for placement in a group because it is difficult to practice peer relationship skills in individual treatment. D is not an appropriate reason for selecting a group member.

Now that Ruth found she needed to operate three groups, and given her already heavily loaded schedule, she looked for potential facilitators among school staff and from the community.

Question: To have the group facilitator reflect the group composition criteria she had used to assemble the groups, she had to consider which of the following descriptive attributes?

A. ___ Gender
B. ___ Race
C. ___ Age

Answer: C would not be a major factor for a facilitator of adolescent groups because every adult will be significantly older than each student. Therefore, the correct answers are A and B.

Ruth's next decision involved whether to have cofacilitators or single facilitators.

Question: Which of the following do you think are advantages of cofacilitators?

A. ___ Cofacilitators can provide different gender and race to match more group members.
B. ___ Cofacilitators can provide more eyes and ears regarding what is going on in a group.
C. ___ Cofacilitators would spend less time planning and reviewing the group's work.
D. ___ Cofacilitators provide different perspectives about goals and issues regarding group meetings.

Answer: A, B, and D clearly point to the strengths of using a cofacilitator plan. C is incorrect because it will take cofacilitators more time to plan meetings and to review what they are experiencing in each group meeting.

Given the three advantages cited in A, B, and D, Ruth decided to have cofacilitators for each group. Through her work in the school and the community, she had developed several relationships with individuals who had indicated an interest in working with groups. This made it possible for her to recruit five individuals who could provide the gender and racial balance she wanted in each pair of group facilitators. Accordingly, because she herself was African American, she recruited

One African American male
One African American female
Two European American males
One European American female

As the final step in composing each group, Ruth assigned her volunteer facilitators as follows:

Sophomore group—nine members[3]
    An African American male
    A European American female
Junior group—nine members
    Ruth (African American female)
    A European American Male
Senior group—seven members
    A European American male
    An African American female

In Chapter 9, we will discuss issues that pertain to planning for a first group meeting and present Ruth's plan for the first meeting of her group.

SUMMARY

In this chapter, we have provided an example of a treatment group whose composition was based on the principles spelled out in the first seven chapters of this book. The group's purpose was based on the results of a questionnaire that sampled concerns of students in one high school. The group's facilitator sought and easily received administrative acceptance of the purpose she chose for the group(s) because the school was accustomed to the use of groups for helping students. She selected grade and race as the critical descriptive attributes and made class grade a common factor for each group, while deliberately mixing the race and gender of members. In selecting facilitators for the group, she chose people of both races (European American and African American) so each group would have a racial mix in adult leadership. She also saw to it that every member had at least one other member in the group who shared attributes of race, grade, and gender. From all of this planning, she hoped to create groups whose members would feel comfortable regarding the group to which they had been assigned.

NOTES

1. As we have said throughout the book, many task and educational groups are composed of individuals who already know one another, prior to the group's first meeting,

but are in a new constellation of people, so that a new group is indeed being created. Nevertheless, in this chapter and in Chapter 9, the example will focus on one kind of group—the treatment group—to demonstrate the major steps in creating a group. It is hoped that these members will leave the first meeting feeling that they are indeed part of a group and are looking forward to the next meeting.

2. Terminology for designating membership based on race remains a sensitive issue. Although "white" and "black" have been used by many authors, current preferred usage for colored/Negro/black individuals appears to be "African American." Accordingly, "European Americans" appears to us to be the appropriate companion for white persons.

3. Ruth added one member to each group—from her own caseload—so that every member would have at least one other member with the same descriptive attribute of race and of gender.

9

PLANNING THE FIRST MEETING

Having settled on the composition of the three groups, Ruth set about making plans for the first group meeting—the one in which she hoped to actually create a group. In conducting this first meeting, she wanted to achieve several outcomes.

- By the end of the meeting, each member would know the first name of every other member.
- By the end of the meeting, each member would be able to describe his or her own role and responsibilities as a member and the general operating procedures of the group.
- By the end of the meeting, each member would have stated—to the group—at least one goal for him or her with regard to his or her participation in this group.
- Each member would leave the meeting with a clear picture of what would happen in the next meeting.
- Each member would plan to return for the next meeting.

Question: Which of the following activities could you use in the first meeting to achieve the outcomes listed previously?

A. ___ Each member would tell his or her life story to the group (short version).

B. ___ Toward the end of the meeting, members would briefly evaluate the meeting itself in terms of what had helped and what might be improved in future meetings.

C. ____ Each member would describe briefly (one or two sentences) at least one relationship he or she hoped to change as a result of being in this group.

D. ____ One member would work—with the group's facilitators and the group—on the relationship he or she hoped to improve, providing a sample of the group in process for all to see.

E. ____ The group would spend most of the session talking about what members wanted to do in future sessions.

F. ____ At the end of the meeting, members would participate in planning the agenda for meeting number 2.

G. ____ Members would spend a majority of the meeting getting acquainted, through informal socializing, while consuming the refreshments that were provided.

With the exception of A (which would take too long), E (which would take time away from the business of this first meeting), and G (a somewhat purposeless use of limited group time), all of the above are activities you could use to enhance the development of this group. Presumably, these are the kinds of activities Ruth and her cofacilitator would use.

To put it more precisely, the following were the steps through which Ruth and her cofacilitator planned to take this group—steps that Ruth had found relevant for most treatment groups during a first meeting:

1. Introduction—of members to one another.
2. Today's agenda—briefly telling members what to expect during this meeting.
3. Contracting—spelling out facilitator and member roles and the operating procedures of the group—for example, confidentiality, widespread participation, member-to-member interaction, and so on.
4. Working—in this meeting, working on the relationship issues of one member, with the group's inputs, as a sample of the group's way of doing things.
5. Reviewing and reflecting—engaging the group in a review of today's meeting—what helped, what else might have been done, and what might be changed. In addition, some feedback would be sought from the one member who had volunteered to ask for the group's help regarding what his or her experience had been like.
6. Next meeting—briefly planning a tentative agenda for meeting number 2.

Let's discuss each of the steps.

INTRODUCTIONS

Question: Assume that you want people to address one another by name. People generally respond better to the use of their name than to a "she said" reference to themselves. Furthermore, assume that the people in a new group are all strangers to one another. Which of the following do you think would work best in terms of helping members use one another's names in the meeting and remembering the names the next time the group meets?

A.＿ With new members seated in a circle, go around the group, and ask each member to pronounce his or her first name slowly and distinctly.

B. ＿ Give out name labels that can be pinned or otherwise attached to one's clothes on which names have been typed (on a typewriter) in capital letters.

C. ＿ Give out name labels that can be pinned or otherwise attached to one's clothes on which each person writes his or her first name, with a thick black felt pen, in large letters.

D.＿ Give each member a 5×8 card, folded lengthwise, and ask each member to write his or her first name on it, in large letters on both surfaces, with a thick black felt pen, then put it down on the table in front of him or her for all to see.

E. ＿ Give each member a blank badge or 5×8 card and tell each member to write his or her name on it with a black felt pen, but to mix up the letters so members will have to guess the correct order. Then make a group game of it, going around the group, with only three guesses to straighten it out. (Your authors could be VHYREA and KNRFA.) If anyone can fool the group, he or she wins a prize.

As you might have guessed, we prefer, C, D, or E. The latter (E) falls under the general category of "icebreaker." (If you use this approach, once everyone's correct name has been guessed, you might revert to a new label, as in alternative C.) In fact, we have often found ourselves in situation B—one that requires farsightedness or up-close viewing that can easily become intrusive! Icebreakers usually take more time than labels but tend to have a more powerful effect on one's memory than the best of labels. Published collections of games often have a chapter on icebreakers (Boyd, 1945/1973, pp. 83-104): Pfeiffer and Jones's (1974) series may be the best source for a wide variety of icebreakers (as well as other group activities). An important ingredient of icebreakers is that they can result in a lot of laughter, which effectively overcomes the tension that often characterizes a first meeting.

Actually, Ruth and her cofacilitator chose a different icebreaking activity for the first meeting. The icebreaker they chose emphasizes active listening by each participant. In this way, they planned to stress listening as a very important part of the future work of all group members.

THE AGENDA

An agenda is a statement of the order of events in a meeting. In any group, the agenda grows out of the group's contract. In a task group, agendas are often created ahead of time so that they can be printed and distributed to members several days before the meeting.

Agendas for treatment and support groups tend to be more informal, but it still helps everyone to know what will be happening during the meeting and in what order.

Because there is so much to accomplish in a first meeting, the agenda must be more structured than it is likely to be for later meetings. In the first meeting, Ruth and her cofacilitator knew that it was their responsibility to draw up the agenda, but subsequently, creating the agenda would be a responsibility shared by Ruth, her coleader, and the members.

Question: Assume that Ruth is presenting the group's agenda after introductions have been completed. Which statement do you think would be most helpful?

A. ___ "In today's meeting, we'll be talking about relationships, and how to improve them."

B. ___ "In today's meeting, we'll talk about our group's contract, your goals for being here, and then we'll work with one member to improve his or her relationship situation."

C. ___ "In today's meeting, we'll first talk about the way our group will work, including what you can expect of us (Ruth and her cofacilitator), and what you should be doing in your role as a group member. We'll next see if you have any questions about the group. Then we'll ask you for one volunteer to work on his or her particular relationship concern, to show you all one of the ways we'll work in here. We'll begin to close the meeting by a review of what we've done, to find out what you found helpful, and what you'd like to see changed in future meetings. Finally, we'll talk briefly about our agenda for our next meeting. Any questions about today's agenda?"

Although C (which we prefer) is considerably longer than B, it provides much more information. Incidentally, people often do not remember what they hear—particularly in a first meeting where members are likely to be anxious—so you can have the agenda written up on a large piece of posterboard or on a chalkboard and refer to it from time to time. In addition, such an easily seen agenda allows members to check out where the group is in its proceedings.[1]

Groups that meet without an agenda often flip-flop all over the place, with no particular sense of direction, and little if anything is accomplished. Accordingly, we favor an explicit agenda shared with all members for any group.

CONTRACTING

Question: Which of the following do you think is the most appropriate definition of the group's contract?

A. ___ A set of guidelines and a definition of the group's purpose stated clearly by the facilitator(s).

B. ___ A set of guidelines and definition of the group's purpose negotiated between the facilitator(s) and the members.

As you may have guessed, we prefer B. Note that the contract is really an agreement that takes shape over the first three or four group meetings because members learn more about the group from experiencing it than from talking about it. One of the rules of the contract is that it is open to renegotiation throughout the life of the group (Croxton, 1985).

An important component of the contract in a treatment group is the goals each member is trying to achieve through his or her participation in this group. We talk a lot about goals, but we often define them poorly.

A well-formed goal statement describes

1. What the person wants to achieve, both in terms of feelings and behavior
2. What will be the outcome when the person gets what he or she wants to achieve

For example, a client had a fear of driving and of having an accident that might hurt someone. He stated his goal initially as (A) "I don't want to be afraid of driving." Somewhat later in the group session, he said, (B) "I want to drive without violating any laws, and I want to own a car." Which statement (A or B) would you consider to be a well-formed goal statement? A is stated in negative terms rather than describing the positive outcome desired.

B is a better approximation of a well-formed goal statement. What it lacks is the outcome that will be achieved when the client gets what he wants.

The client finally completed his goal statement when he said, "I want to own a car and drive it safely, so that I can feel that I am an adult."

This well-formed goal statement includes the positive actions involved in getting what is wanted (i.e., buying a car and driving the car safely) and the feelings the actions will provide (feeling like an adult).

Question: Which of the following goal statements are well formed?

A. ___ "I want to feel less depressed."

B. ___ "I would like things to go better between me and my mom and dad."

C. ___ "I want to talk more often with my dad, so that I can know more about his thinking. In that way, I can feel as if we are really communicating."

D. ___ "I want some new friends."

Answer: C is the better formed statement. A is negatively stated—we prefer goals that are stated in positive terms. B is not specific—that is, it would be hard to measure whether or not it had been achieved to any significant degree. It needs an action verb. C is a good statement—although it could use a little more specificity. D does not have the outcome described and contains no action verb, so we do not see it as an appropriate goal statement.

During the first meeting, the facilitator helps each member develop a tentative goal for himself or herself.[2]

The contract should also include some of the group's rules—for example, "What's said in meetings is not to be repeated outside of meetings"—and an explanation of how the group will operate—for example, "Sometimes we'll work with one member for awhile, and sometimes we'll deal with an issue that has been proving difficult for several of you. In spelling out our agenda for a meeting, we should all know which topic we are dealing with at any given time," and so on.

WORKING

Thanks to the screening interviews, Ruth and her coleader had considerable information about the relationships that were proving difficult for each member. The issues the members faced were, as she expected, quite different, although there were some underlying commonalities. To try to deal with all of them at any single meeting would be, they believed, impossible. Accordingly, she and her cofacilitator decided to focus the group on one member's concerns for 15 to 20 minutes.

There are a great many different approaches to working with people in groups. In *Models of Group Therapy,* Shaffer and Galinsky (1989) describe 12 different models, each of which has its own literature and its own inspirational authors. Over the years, the models have become less distinct as practitioners are influenced by the writings of various authors and borrow ideas and techniques from the various approaches. Although Ruth had been educated in a graduate school of social work, her approach to working with groups had changed over the years partially because she had to learn to survive in the reality of practice and partially from reading about the work of various group work authors. She was no longer sure what name to apply to what she did, but she had developed confidence in her effectiveness as a group worker. Working with an individual member while the other members watched was one way she had learned to be effective.

Question: While working with one member, as the other members watched, what do you think they would be doing?

A. ___ Daydreaming

B. ___ Resting

C. ___ Observing

D. ___ Listening

E. ___ Mentally applying what was being discussed to their own situations

F. ___ Participating from time to time

G. ___ Watching Ruth and her cofacilitator to see how one can be helpful

Actually, probably all of the above could be considered correct, but we prefer everything from C on down. In future meetings, Ruth and her cofacilitator might focus the group's attention on an issue with which they all deal, such as how to manage one's anger, what to do after a blowup has occurred, how to start a conversation and head it in a positive direction, and so on. For this first meeting, however, she wanted to demonstrate how she and her cofacilitator would work with one member at a time, serving as the primary helpers, with occasional inputs from the other members. As the group moved through future meetings, she expected that members would assume the role of primary helper for one another, or cohelper roles, with Ruth and her cofacilitator moving into more of an observer-guider role.

REVIEWING AND REFLECTING

Before ending the meeting, Ruth and her cofacilitator wanted to ask the helpseeker to share some of his or her internal thoughts and feelings that had occurred during the helping session.

Question: Which of the following questions from Ruth or her cofacilitator do you think would be helpful to the helpseeker? (Remember that these questions are hypothetical: Some of them are questions they would never ask.)

A. ____ "What did you find helpful, and what was not helpful?"

B. ____ "Do you feel you made progress toward achieving your goal?"

C. ____ "Does anyone in the group have a solution to the helpseeker's questions that they would like to share now?"

D. ____ "What strengths did you notice in the helpseeker while he or she was working with us?"

E. ____ "What mistakes did we (Ruth and her cofacilitator) make?"

F. ____ "What changes did you see in the helpseeker as the helping progressed, either in the words he or she used or in his or her nonverbal cues?"

G. ____ "Did you think the helpseeker was being honest?"

The difficulty with C is that it could open up the discussion once again, rather than providing feedback to the helpseeker on how he or she participated in the working session. Response E shifts the focus to Ruth and her cofacilitator, which at this point is not what the feedback is about. G implies the possibility that the helpseeker was lying or at least not telling everything. Although it is possible that someone might cover up in a first meeting (when trust has not yet been established), responding to this question in a negative way could leave a bad taste in the helpseeker's mouth, and he or she might not return. In addition, other members would be discouraged from playing the helpseeker's role in future meetings. The other two questions are more likely to elicit supportive comments, rewarding the helpseeker for volunteering.

The second part of the reviewing or reflecting segment of the meeting is an open, relatively unstructured sharing of the thoughts and feelings each participant experienced during the working session.

Question: Which of the following questions would you use to elicit these thoughts or feelings?

A. ___ "What impact did our words have on each of you?"

B. ___ "Does anyone have anything to say about the working session?"

C. ___ "Imagine that the meeting is over and you're having lunch with your best friend. What would you tell him or her?"

D. ___ "What was different about this problem solving from other times when any of you have talked about your problems?"

Answer: Question A seeks the internal experience of each participant to move toward being comfortable in sharing internal thoughts or feelings. We think it could be helpful.

Question B is a closed question that tends to shut off open sharing because it can be answered with a yes or no, so we suggest that it should not be asked.

Question C inappropriately suggests breaking confidentiality about what happened in the group so we would not ask it.

Question D may elicit how this session differed from a "gripe" session, thus building confidence that real change can occur through the helping process in this group, so we might use it.

Question: The last stage Ruth and her cofacilitator wanted to reach during the first session was to briefly plan the next session. Which of the following statements could they use to accomplish that task?

A. ___ "Who would like to be the helpseeker next week?"

B. ___ "Remember, everything that was said in here is confidential and not to be repeated to anyone who is not in this group."

C. ___ "We'll start out next week listening to our audiotape of this working session, so you can help us identify some things we did

that you thought were helpful, and some things that could have
been handled differently."

D. ___ "We'll use the same structure next week, and then you can let
us know how you might like to change some of the ways we all
work together."

Answer: We would not use statement A because it puts too much pressure
on someone over the week thinking about being the focus of the next
meeting. It is better to have the helpseeker volunteer at the key moment in
the meeting. Ruth and her cofacilitator can also listen carefully to members
as they enter the meeting room and when they are speaking during the early
group activity. Members often let clues slip out about their high motivation
to deal with something during the times when there is little pressure (i.e.,
during the informal moments of a meeting) to participate.

Statement B is an important reminder regarding building trust about
exposure in group meetings. We would use it, unless it sounds like an
admonition to members who already have this message about how to give
help.

Statement C is an excellent way to build on the learning that occurred
during the first session—about how to give help. The only problem is that
it may take up too much time. If you use this approach, you might do well
to preselect a short portion of the tape for review.

Statement D is an excellent message intended to empower members to
influence the way the group will function in the future.

SUMMARY

In this chapter, we have focused on the steps to follow during a first
meeting that we think will help create a group to which members will want
to return for future meetings. Summarizing briefly, in a first meeting you
want to

1. Facilitate the introduction of members to one another.
2. Spell out the agenda for this first meeting.
3. Negotiate an initial contract with the members concerning the individual and
   group goals and roles for this group.
4. Do some "group work" to set the model for future meetings.
5. Involve the members in an evaluation of the meeting.
6. Involve everyone in setting a tentative agenda for the next meeting.

IN CLOSING

This book has been designed to help you become familiar with the range of considerations and activities involved in beginning to work with a group. As such, it has focused on the initial components of the group work process. Obviously, there is much more to be learned about effective group work. We believe, however, in the old motto, "Well begun is half done." Many groups fail because the basic processes involved in group creation have been mismanaged. We hope this book will help you to create groups that produce results that—in time—become satisfying and productive for all involved. Good luck with your groups!

NOTES

1. In an educational group, agenda creation may well be the facilitator's role throughout the life of the group, but the facilitator should begin each session by informing the group of the agenda for today and take their needs into account when establishing the agenda. Sometimes a support group's agenda is simply to go around the circle of those attending and have each report on his or her current situation, including requests for help from the group. It is not very fancy, but it is an agenda nonetheless. In such a situation, it is the facilitator's role to see to it that no one member takes an inappropriately large amount of the group's time.

2. This same kind of specificity can be used in a task group but the focus should be on achieving the group's goals. In an educational group, the facilitator often has individual goals for each participant but makes no assumption that members will help one another to achieve these goals. When and if this happens, it is often the result of an informal contract between some members of the educational group and often takes place outside of the group unless the instructor builds such subgroup goals into the instructional process. Goals for support group members operate very much like those for the members of a treatment group.

CLOSING POEM

In creating a group,
You want to take care
That the folks you invite
All want to be there.
That the group's raison d'être
Is in tune with their needs,
And its mixture of members
Will enhance their group's deeds.
Empowering members
Helps each of them feel
That this group's truly theirs,
And that *that* is for real.
You'll want to attend
To time, size, and space,
These issues need thought,
Don't treat them with haste.
When you've done or thought through
All the items above,
You're set to get started,
So go to it, my love.
And as this book ends,
And you're off on your own,
Remember these words,
And engrave them in stone,
We think they'll be helpful,
(Since you'll soon be begun)
In doing a job
That should prove to be fun.
So good luck to you all,
As you cre-*ate* your troop,
Carry on, and enjoy,
When you work with your group!

REFERENCES

Bales, R. (1950). *Interaction process analysis: A method for the study of small groups.* Reading, MA: Addison-Wesley.

Bales, R., & Cohen, S. (1979). *SYMLOG: A system for the multiple level observation of groups.* New York: Free Press.

Bell, J. (1995). Traumatic event debriefing: Service delivery designs and the role of social work. *Social Work, 40*(1), 36-43.

Bertcher, H. (1994). *Group participation techniques for leaders and members* (2nd ed.). Thousand Oaks, CA: Sage.

Boyd, N. (1973). *Handbook of recreational games.* New York: Dover. (Original work published 1945)

Brown, A., & Mistry, T. (1994). Group work with "mixed membership" groups: Issues of race and gender. *Social Work With Groups, 17*(3), 5-21.

Croxton, T. (1985). The therapeutic contract. In M. Sundel, P. Glasser, R. Sarri, & R. Vinter (Eds.), *Individual change through small groups* (2nd ed., pp. 159-179). New York: Free Press.

Cyberspace. (1995, Spring). *Time* [Special issue], p. 24.

Davis, L. (1995). The crisis of diversity. In *Capturing the power of diversity* (pp. 47-57). New York: Haworth.

Evans, R., & Jaureguy, B. (1981). Group therapy by phone: A cognitive behavioral program for visually impaired elderly. *Social Work in Health Care, 7,* 79-91.

Evans, R., Smith, K., Werkhoven, W., Fox, H., & Pritzl, D. (1986). Cognitive telephone group therapy with physically disabled elderly persons. *The Gerontologist, 26*(1), 8-10.

Fatout, M., & Rose, S. (1995). *Task groups in the social services.* Thousand Oaks, CA: Sage.

Finn, J., & Lavitt, M. (1994). Computer-based self-help groups for sexual abuse survivors. *Social Work With Groups, 17*(1/2), 21-46.

Forsyth, D. (1990). *Group dynamics* (2nd ed.). Pacific Grove, CA: Brooks/Cole.

Lauffer, A. (1978). *Doing continuing education and staff development.* New York: McGraw-Hill.

Pfeiffer, J., & Jones, J. (1974). *Structured experiences for human relations training: A reference guide* (Vols. 1-5). La Jolla, CA: University Associates.

Rittner, B., & Hammons, K. (1993). Telephone group work with end stage AIDS. *Social Work With Groups, 15*(4), 59-72.

Shaffer, J., & Galinsky, M. D. (1989). *Models of group therapy* (2nd ed.). Englewood Cliffs, NJ: Prentice Hall.

Toseland, R., & Siporin, M. (1986). When to recommend group treatment: A review of the clinical and research literature. *International Journal of Group Psychotherapy, 36*(2), 171-201.

Trang, T., & Urbano, J. (1993). A telephone support program for the visually impaired elderly. *Clinical Gerontologist, 13*(2), 61-71.

University of Michigan, Information Technology Division. (1994). *Online Directory Services—X-500 User Overview* (rev. ed., Reference No. R1124). Ann Arbor, MI: Author.

Yalom, I. (1983). *Inpatient group psychotherapy.* New York: Basic Books.

ABOUT THE AUTHORS

Harvey J. Bertcher is retired as Professor of Social Work at the University of Michigan School of Social Work. He has considerable experience in social work with groups, including work in residential and day treatment centers, street gang work, settlement houses and community centers, and group work with ex-psychiatric hospital patients and handicapped children. In recent years, he has taken leadership in the development of group work by telephone using conference-calling technology. He has served as consultant to human service agencies, including 3 years as the National Consultant in Social Work to the Office of the Surgeon General, the U.S. Air Force. He has coauthored several volumes, including *Creating Groups* (with Frank Maple) and *Role Modeling, Role Playing* (with Jesse Gordon et al.). He is also the author of *Staff Development in Human Service Organizations* and *Group Participation: Techniques for Leaders and Members.*

Frank F. Maple is Professor of Social Work at the University of Michigan School of Social Work. In his current position, he specializes in the use of technology for the teaching/learning process in methods classes on interviewing, group work, and family therapy. He has published six software programs titled *Goal-Focused Therapy* and has produced five interactive videodiscs under the same title. His other publications include *Shared Decision Making* and *Dynamic Interviewing: An Introduction to Counseling,* and he is the coeditor (with Rosemary Sarri) of *The School in the Community.*

ADV 3274